Canadian Curriculum SummerSmart 2·3

Credits

Photos (Front Cover "children" Gennadiy Poznyakov/123RF.com, "beach toys" serezniy/123RF.com, "beach" Alexandr Ozerov/123RF.com. Back Cover "children" Anatoliy Samara/123RF.com, "school bus" Thomas Bedenk/123RF.com, "children" Dmitriy Shironosov/123RF.com, "classroom" Franck Boston/123RF.com, "girl looking at grass" Sergiy Bykhunenko/123RF.com, "girl blowing windmill" Logos/123RF.com, "bee" szefei/123RF.com, "lorikeets" Tyler Panian/123RF.com, "children" Anatoliy Samara/123RF.com, "Chateau Frontenac" Susan Peterson/123RF.com)

Printed in China

ISBN: 978-1-77149-144-0

Contents

Grades 2–3

Week

ISBN: 978-1-77149-144-0

Week

ISBN: 978-1-77149-144-0

Dear Parent:

While all work and no play makes Jack a dull boy, all play and no work would probably make Jack forget most of what he has learned, which is why it is necessary to schedule regular practice in the long summer vacation to help your child consolidate what he or she has learned.

This is where Canadian Curriculum SummerSmart can help.

Canadian Curriculum SummerSmart provides practice for your child to review the essentials taught in the previous academic year and prepares him or her for the grade ahead with confidence. The series is organized in an easy-to-use format: each title is made up of eight weeks (units) of work so your child can complete one unit each week during the summer vacation. The units are comprised of practice in English, Math, Science, and Social Studies. Engaging Arts and Crafts activities, as well as Comics and Fun Places to Go in Summer, are also included for added fun.

Your child will be delighted to have Canadian Curriculum SummerSmart as his or her summer learning buddy.

Your Partner in Education,
Popular Book Company (Canada) Limited

ISBN: 978-1-77149-144-0

Week 1

English

- read a story
- give examples of items
- identify words that rhyme
- make compound words
- complete a word search

Mathematics

- do addition and subtraction
- solve word problems
- complete and describe patterns

Science

- explore the animal groups
- learn how animals adapt to their environment

Social Studies

- learn about family roles in the past and present
- learn about objects and their uses in the past and present

ISBN: 978-1-77149-144-0

A. Read the paragraphs about popcorn. Then check ✓ the true sentences.

Popcorn

It's white! It's fluffy! It smells and tastes great! It's popcorn!

Most people love to eat popcorn. It is made when a kernel of corn gets hot and pops into a fluffy snack. A popular way to eat popcorn is with melted butter, but this snack comes in many delicious flavours.

Popcorn has been around for a very long time. Native Americans ate popcorn and used it to decorate their ceremonial headdresses, necklaces, and ornaments.

1. Kernels pop when they get hot. ◯
2. Butter melts popcorn. ◯
3. Popcorn smells great but tastes bad. ◯
4. Popcorn comes in many different flavours. ◯
5. Native Americans knew how to make popcorn. ◯
6. Native Americans liked to make decorations and ornaments with popcorn. ◯

ISBN: 978-1-77149-144-0

B. Give an example of each item.

1. another popular snack like popcorn ________________
2. a place where people eat popcorn ________________
3. something that is fluffy like popcorn ________________
4. something white like popcorn ________________
5. your favourite flavour of popcorn ________________

C. Trace the words that rhyme with "hot" with a red pencil and the words that rhyme with "pop" with a blue one.

ISBN: 978-1-77149-144-0

D. **Match the words to make compound words.**

Compound Words

pop bed
basket back rain
cup eye camp

+

corn coat
lid room site
ball pack cake

popcorn ______ ______
______ ______
______ ______
______ ______

E. **Add words to make compound words.**

1.

sun______

sun______

sun______

2.

book______

book______

book______

ISBN: 978-1-77149-144-0

F. Circle the words in the word search.

f	s	j	r	e	c									
b	n	y	q	i	p									
c	a	r	t	w	n	y								
k	c	a	r	a	m	e	l	e						
b	k	c	a	h	w	s	i	n	d	t	y	n	b	i
h	c	h	e	e	s	e	n	q	f	q	h	f	w	j
h	n	q	g	b	f	p	b	d	l	h	t	i	k	t
	e	k	e	r	n	e	l	h	a	e	f	w	g	a
	b	t	h	m	w	t	e	b	v	w	n	b	y	s
p	o	p	c	o	r	n	n	w	o	q	f	k	q	t
g	w	v	b	v	w	t	y	r	u	e	b	w	i	y
t	p	j	d	i	z	s	e	g	r	a	i	n	e	g
w	h	i	t	e	b	f	q	n	b	m	n	w		
f	g	z	i	b	u	s	b	u	t	t	e	r		
			n	p	e	b	e	f	l	j	n	b	m	i
			g	q	v	f	l	u	f	f	y	w	a	q

ISBN: 978-1-77149-144-0

A. Do the addition and subtraction to find the highways the school bus driver has to take to reach the farm. Trace the route on the map.

1. $16 + 23 =$

2. $75 - 9 =$

3. $21 + 19 =$

4. $54 - 7 =$

5. $69 - 18 =$

6. $17 + 17 =$

7.

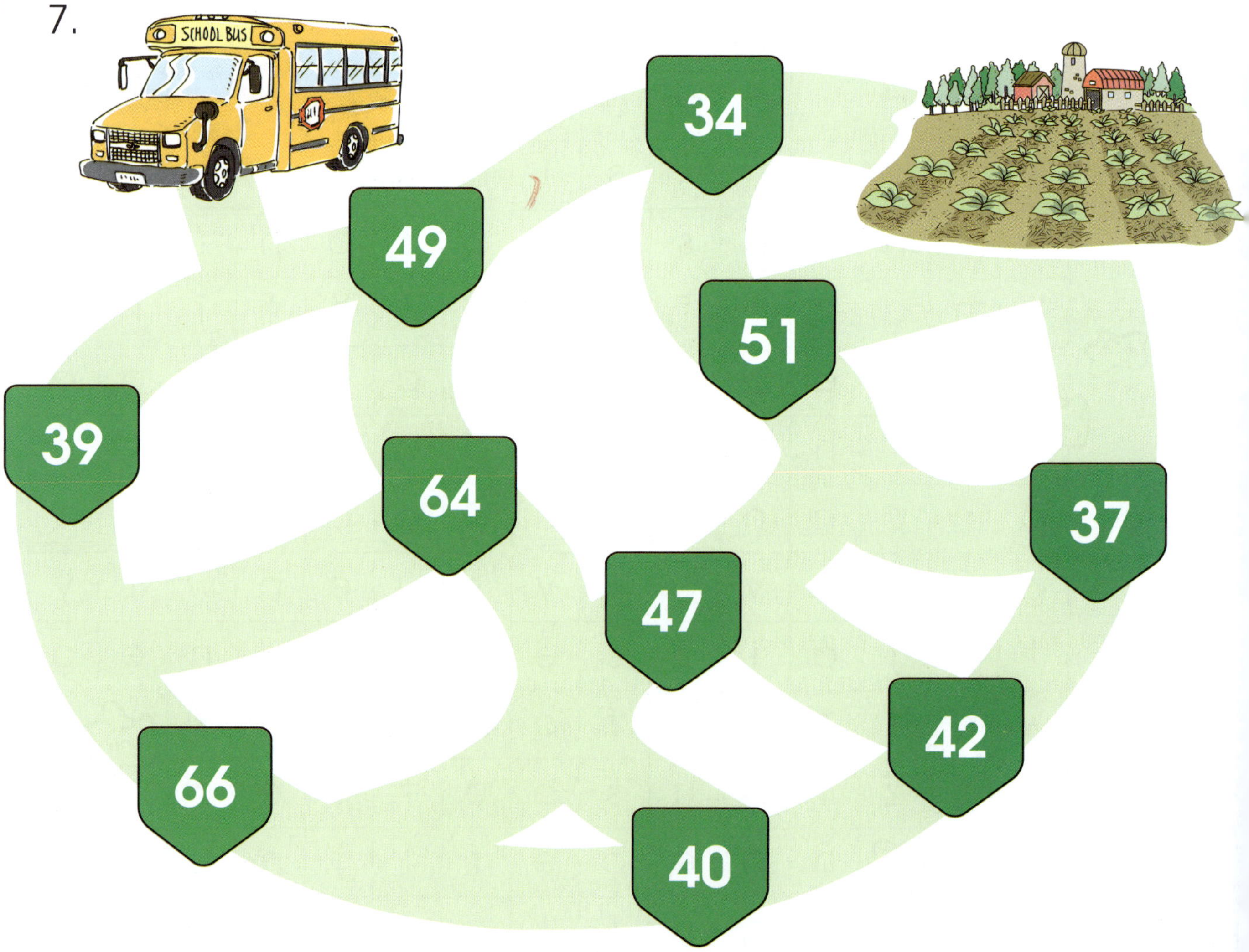

ISBN: 978-1-77149-144-0

B. Solve the problems.

1. There are 19 grade 1 students and 24 grade 2 students on the bus.

a. How many students are there in all?

_____ ◯ _____ = _____

There are _____ students in all.

b. There are 26 girls on the bus. How many boys are there?

_____ ◯ _____ = _____

There are _____ boys.

2. There are 2 bags, each containing 28 cookies.

a. How many cookies are there in all?

_____ ◯ _____ = _____

There are _____ cookies in all.

b. If each child on the bus gets a cookie, how many cookies will be left?

_____ ◯ _____ = _____

_____ cookies will be left.

ISBN: 978-1-77149-144-0

C. Look at the food items. Fill in the blanks.

1. 

4 children share 8 cupcakes. Each child gets ________ cupcakes.

2. 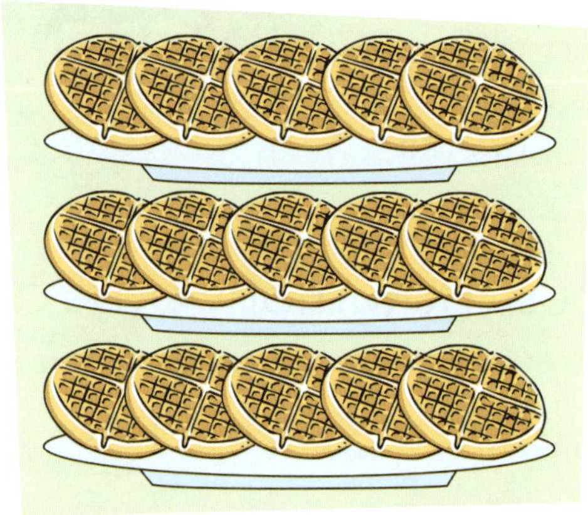

Each plate has 5 waffles. There are ________ waffles in all on 3 plates.

3. 

Each pie has 6 slices. 4 pies have ________ slices in all.

4. 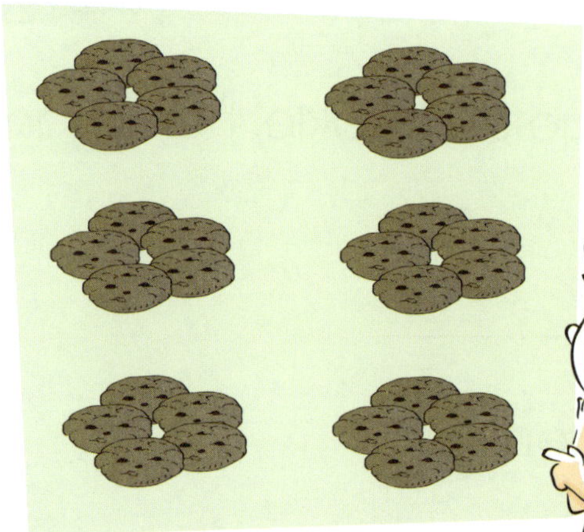

6 children share 30 cookies. Each child gets ________ cookies.

ISBN: 978-1-77149-144-0

D. Draw the picture that comes next in each pattern. Then describe the pattern.

A

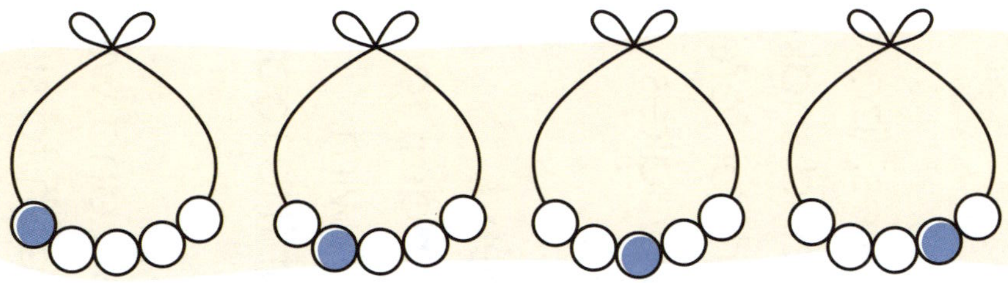

Pattern: ______________________________

B

Pattern: ______________________________

ISBN: 978-1-77149-144-0

A. Draw lines to match the clues with the animal groups.

Different animals have different physical and behavioural characteristics.

mammal

fish

bird

amphibian

reptile

Water or land,
Fur or hair.
We feed milk to our young
And breathe only air.

Underwater,
Gills and fins.
Upstream, downstream,
Scaly skin.

Crocodiles, lizards,
Turtles, and snakes.
In deserts or forests,
In seas or lakes.

Frog, newt,
Salamander, toad.
First we swim,
Then hit the road.

Feathers and wings,
From earth to sky.
We hatch from eggs
And most of us fly.

ISBN: 978-1-77149-144-0

B. Fill in the blanks. Then match the animals to show how they adapt to their environment.

migrate camouflage hibernate

1. c________________ : blend into the surroundings

   h________________ : minimize activities during winter months

   m________________ : travel from one place to another

2.

ISBN: 978-1-77149-144-0

Week 1

Social Studies

A. **Fill in the blanks to learn about family roles in the past. Then draw and write about the roles in your family.**

Roles in the Past

protect
nuts
wood
fishing

I take my older boys hunting and 1. ____________ . We also 2. ____________ our family.

My daughters and I collect wild berries, 3. ____________ , and vegetables.

I respect the adults in my father's clan and collect 4. ____________ for fire.

Roles in My Family

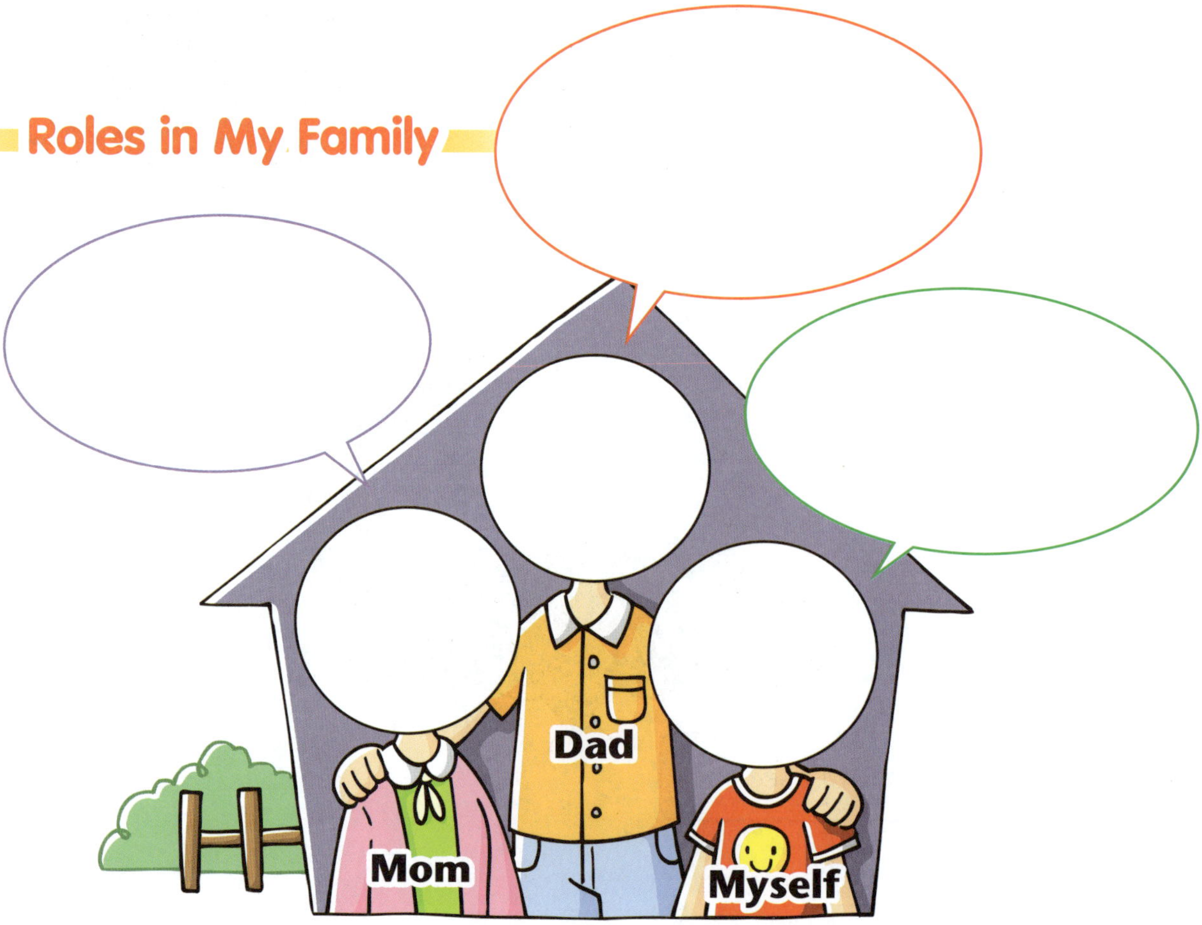

ISBN: 978-1-77149-144-0

B. **Draw the pictures in the correct boxes to complete the table.**

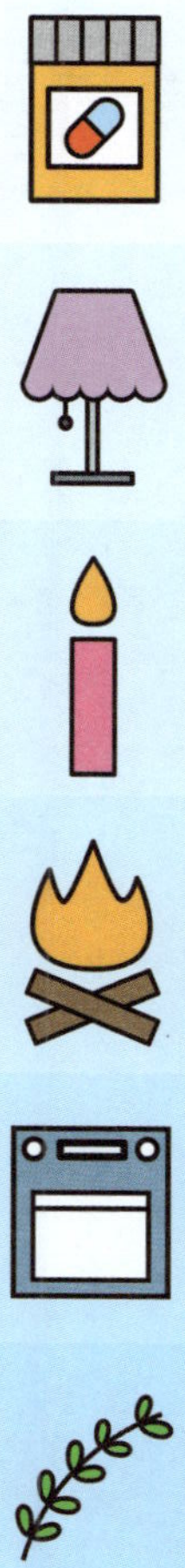

medicine

lamp

candle

fire

stove

herbs

Things of the Past and Present

Used by...		Used for...
The First Nations in the Past	Families in the Present	
		cooking
		providing light
		healing the sick

ISBN: 978-1-77149-144-0

ISBN: 978-1-77149-144-0

WEEK 2

English

- read a poem
- identify rhyming words
- write questions for an interview
- follow instructions to complete a picture
- write sentences using descriptive words

Mathematics

- identify the shapes that belong to the same group
- name some solids and learn their characteristics
- draw the line of symmetry
- complete patterns and name the shapes used to create them

Science

- learn the characteristics of living things
- name animals and their babies

Social Studies

- learn about the ways early Canadians travelled
- learn about birchbark canoes

ISBN: 978-1-77149-144-0

A. Read the poem. Circle the things that make Chuckles odd-looking. Then check ✔ the correct answers.

Chuckles the Clown

Chuckles the Clown is an odd-looking fellow.
He wears a red nose and a hat that is yellow.

His shoes are too big.
His hair is a wig.

His face is a painted smile.
The baggy clothes are way out of style.

Although he looks funny,
He makes a cloudy day sunny.

Chuckles the Clown
Is a hit in this town.

1. "Odd-looking" means
   - (A) looking strange.
   - (B) looking happy.
   - (C) looking sad.

2. "Hit" means
   - (A) failure.
   - (B) success.
   - (C) king.

ISBN: 978-1-77149-144-0

B. Find the words in the poem that rhyme with the words below.

1. ______ **wig** | **town** 2. ______

3. ______ **stay** | **space** 4. ______

5. ______ **sunny** | **yellow** 6. ______

C. You have been asked to interview Chuckles the Clown. Write three questions that you would like to ask him on the given topics.

____

____

____

____

____

____

ISBN: 978-1-77149-144-0

Week 2

English

D. Follow the instructions to complete the picture.

1. Give your clown a silly name.
2. Draw curly green hair for the clown.
3. Draw a hat for the clown's head. Colour it purple.
4. Colour the clown's nose red.
5. Colour the clown's shoes blue.
6. Colour the clown's stripes purple and orange.
7. Draw three balloons on the strings in the clown's hand.

Name : ______________________________

ISBN: 978-1-77149-144-0

E. Enrich the sentences with descriptive words.

Example

The clowns are teasing each other.

The funny clowns are teasing each other.

1. The children are holding balloons.

    ____

2. Chuckles the Clown has a dog.

    ____

3. The dog is wearing a cap.

    ____

4. Have you seen a dog on a scooter?

    ____

5. Each child received a bag of snacks.

    ____

6. The girl is jumping through a hoop.

    ____

ISBN: 978-1-77149-144-0

A. **Colour the shapes that belong in each group. Then name the type of shape for each group.**

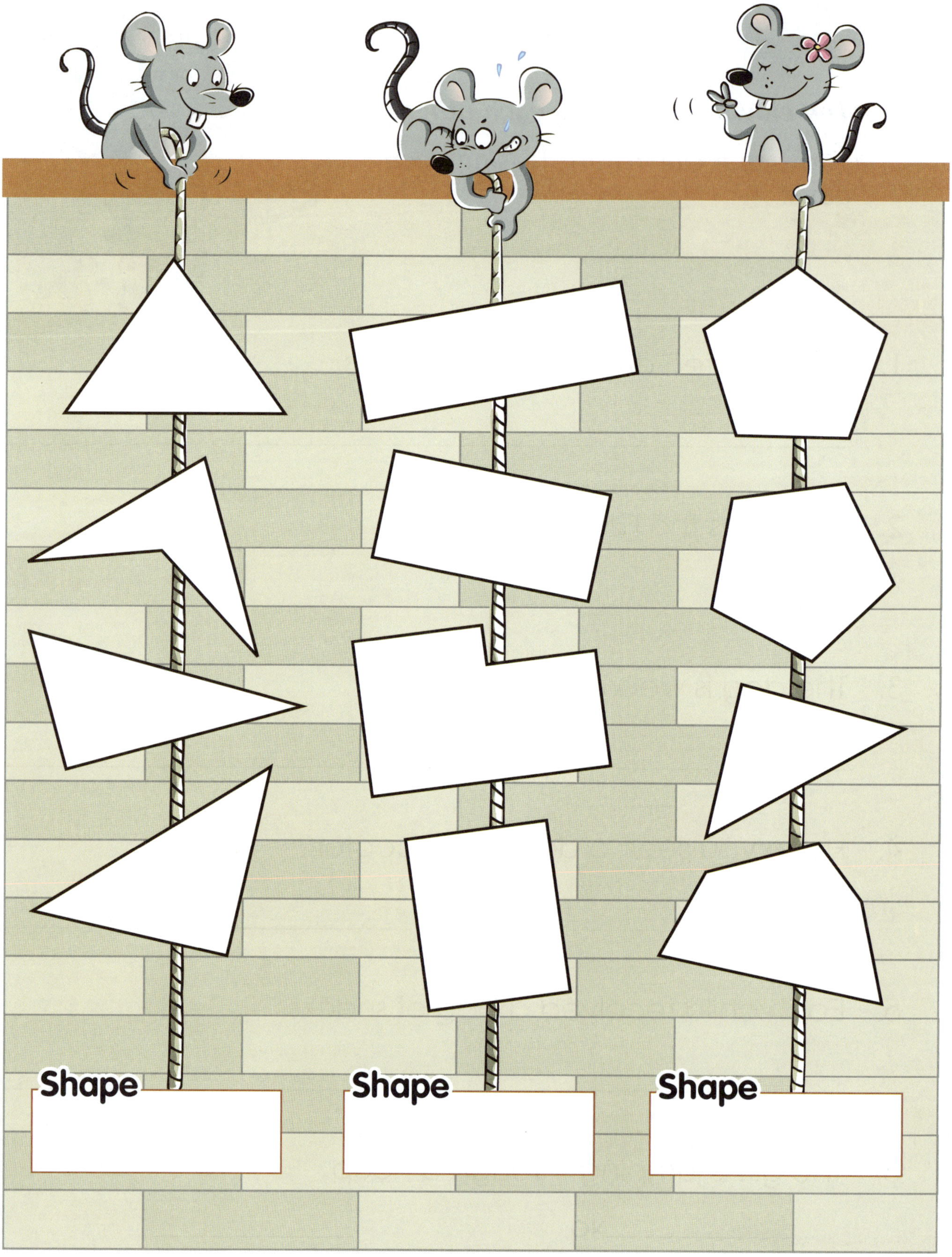

ISBN: 978-1-77149-144-0

B. Draw lines to complete the drawings. Name the solids and circle the correct answers.

1.

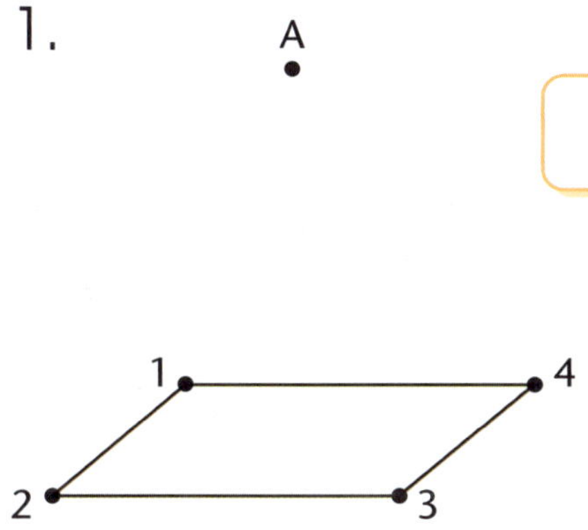

Name: ________________

Is it stackable? **Yes / No**

2.

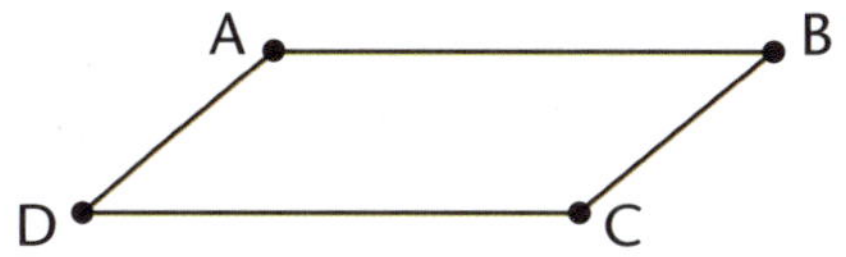

Name: ________________

Can it roll? **Yes / No**

3.

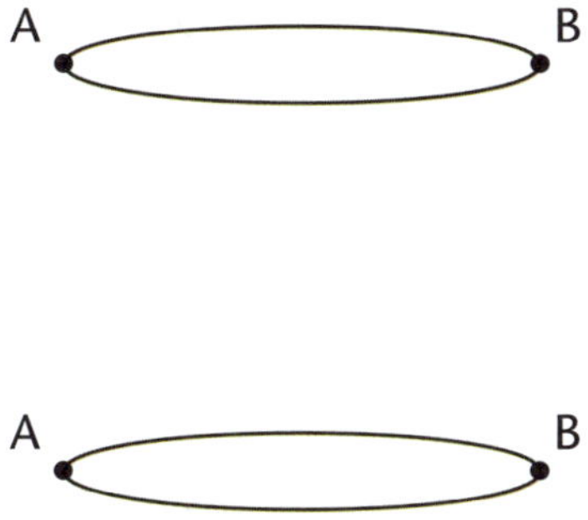

Name: ________________

Can it roll? **Yes / No**

4.

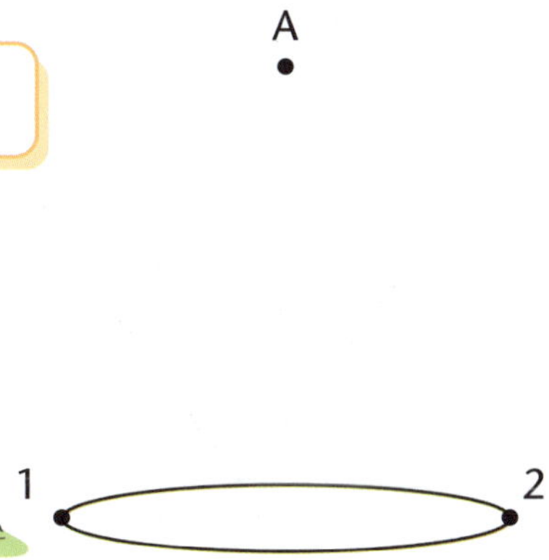

Name: ________________

Is it stackable?

Yes / No

ISBN: 978-1-77149-144-0

C. See how each shape is cut out from the folded paper. Colour the correct cut-out and draw a line of symmetry on it.

1.

2.

3.

4.

ISBN: 978-1-77149-144-0

D. Complete each pattern. Then name the shapes used in the pattern.

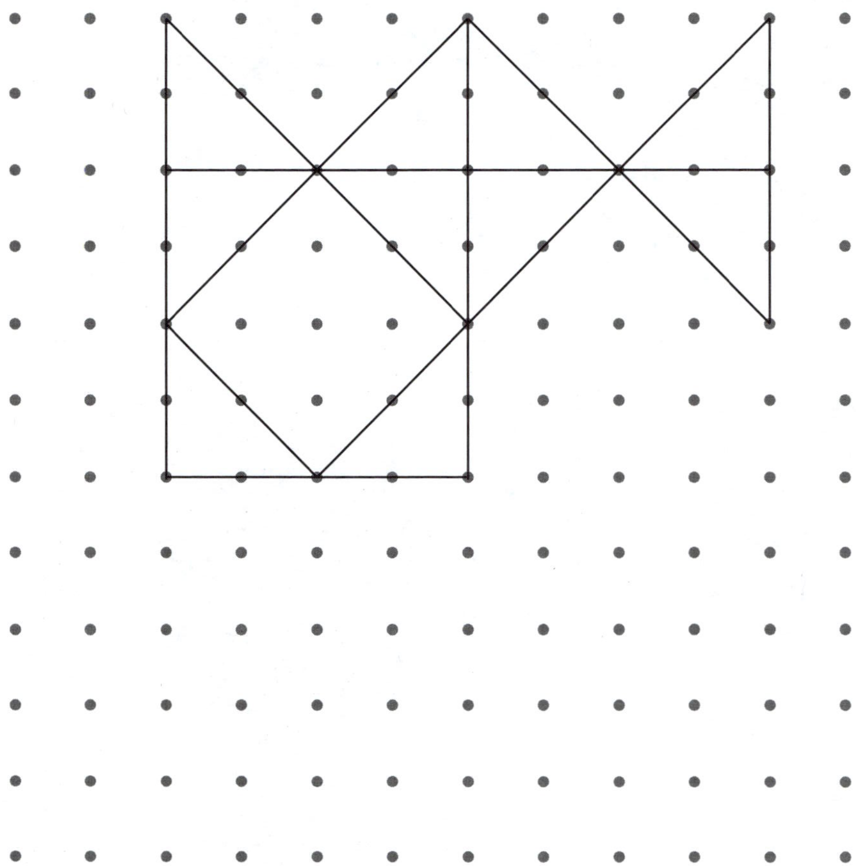

Shapes Used

- ______________________
- ______________________

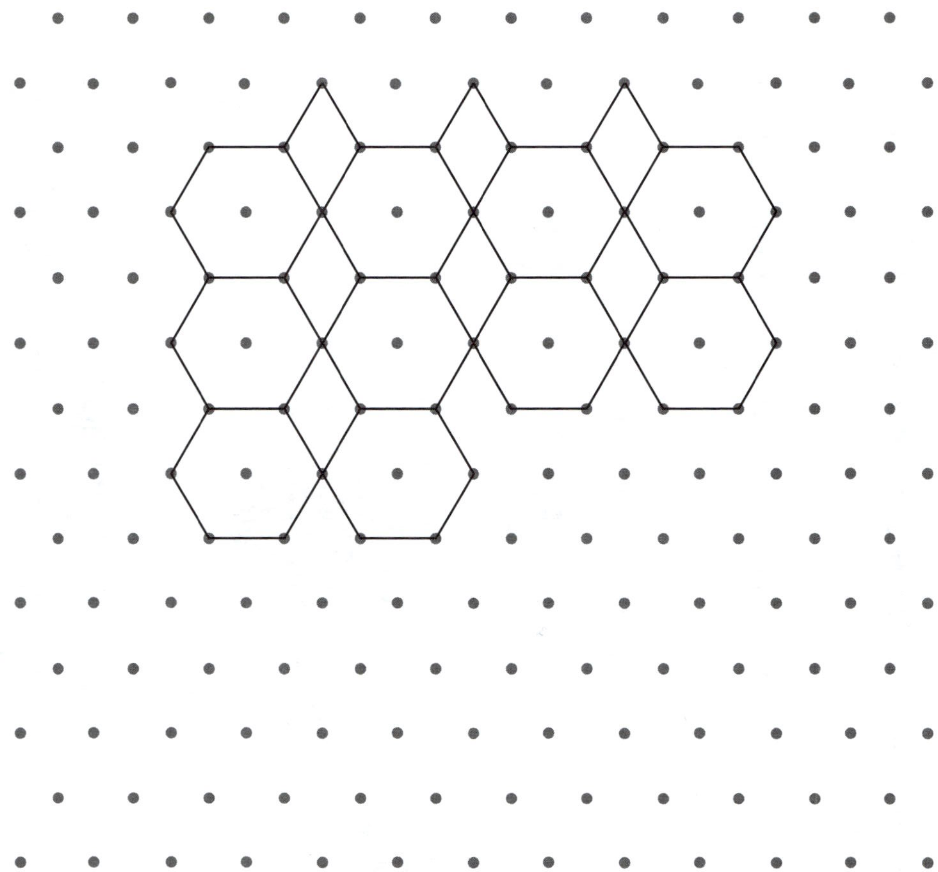

Shapes Used

- ______________________
- ______________________

ISBN: 978-1-77149-144-0

A. Fill in the blanks to show the characteristics of living things.

waste   reproduce   change   food   grow

Characteristics of **Living Things**

1.

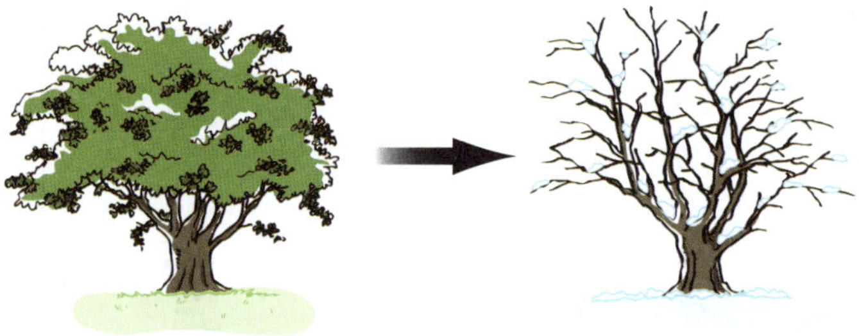

__________ with their surroundings

2.

produce __________

3.

____

4.

consume __________

5.

____

ISBN: 978-1-77149-144-0

B. Name the animals and their babies.

Mammals are born live instead of hatching from eggs. Their babyhood names differ from their adult names.

		Baby		Adult
piglet pig	1.	fawn		deer
bear cub	2.	kitten		cat
cow calf	3.	calf		cow
cat kitten	4.	piglet		pig
fawn deer	5.	kid		goat
goat kid	6.	cub		bear

ISBN: 978-1-77149-144-0

A. Draw lines to show how the early Canadians travelled.

The Early Canadians

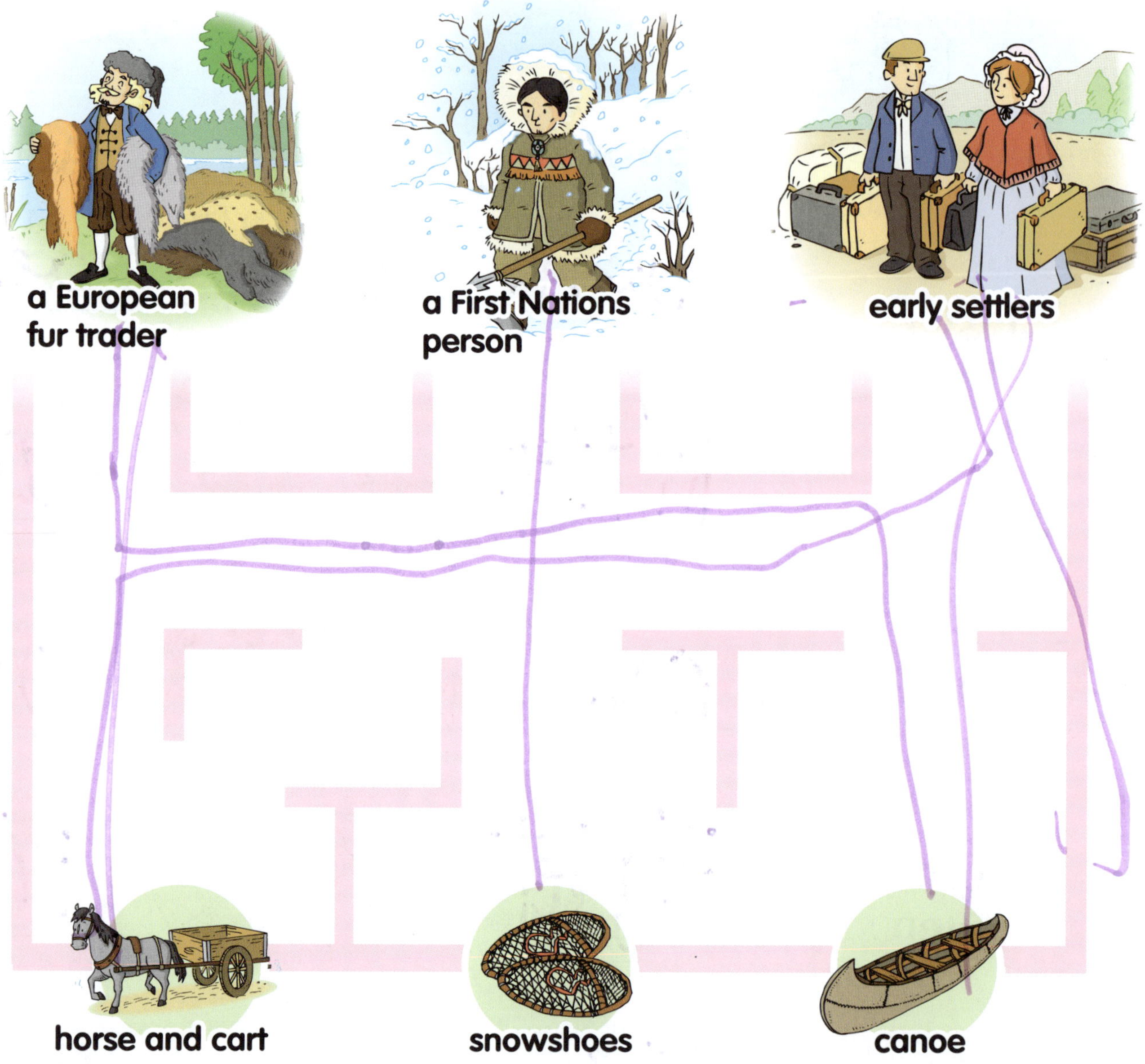

How is your way of travelling different from those of the early Canadians?

ISBN: 978-1-77149-144-0

B. Fill in the blanks to learn more about the birchbark canoe. Then circle the correct words.

The Birchbark Canoe –
an Important Means of Transportation

Canada bark loads

The canoe is able to carry heavy 1. ____________ of animal fur for trading.

This type of canoe was used by the early settlers to travel across 2. ____________ .

The canoe is made from the 3. ____________ of birch trees.

Properties of Birch Trees:

The properties of birch trees are perfect for making canoes.

- The bark comes off in **big / small** pieces.
- The bark is **heavy / lightweight** .
- Birch trees grow **abundantly / scarcely** in Canada.

ISBN: 978-1-77149-144-0

ISBN: 978-1-77149-144-0

Week 3

English
- solve riddles
- write similes
- complete a crossword puzzle

Mathematics
- learn about capacity
- write fractions
- answer questions about probability

Science
- name the three states of water
- learn about cloud formation

Social Studies
- learn about French and British settlers
- learn about Canada's identity
- learn about celebrations in Canada

ISBN: 978-1-77149-144-0

A. Read the clues and solve the riddle.

Riddle Fun

I was invented many years ago.

River ice was used to make me.

I am made with ice and milk.

I am kept in the freezer.

I am served for dessert.

I come in many delicious flavours.

Sometimes I am scooped onto a cone.

What am I?

Guess

____

ISBN: 978-1-77149-144-0

B. Draw your own super ice cream sundae. Give it a catchy name. Then complete the similes.

1.

2. Ice cream is as cold as ______________________________ .

3. Chocolate sauce is like ______________________________ .

4. Milk is as ______________________________ .

5. The vanilla flavour is like ______________________________ .

6. The nuts are as ______________________________ .

ISBN: 978-1-77149-144-0

C. Read the clues and complete the crossword puzzle.

Across

A. Hot Fudge ____

B. ____ Chip (a flavour of ice cream)

C. milk____ (a cold drink)

D. birthday ____ and ice cream

Down

1. ____ Road (a flavour of ice cream)
2. flavoured ice on a stick
3. ice cream ____
4. ____ cone

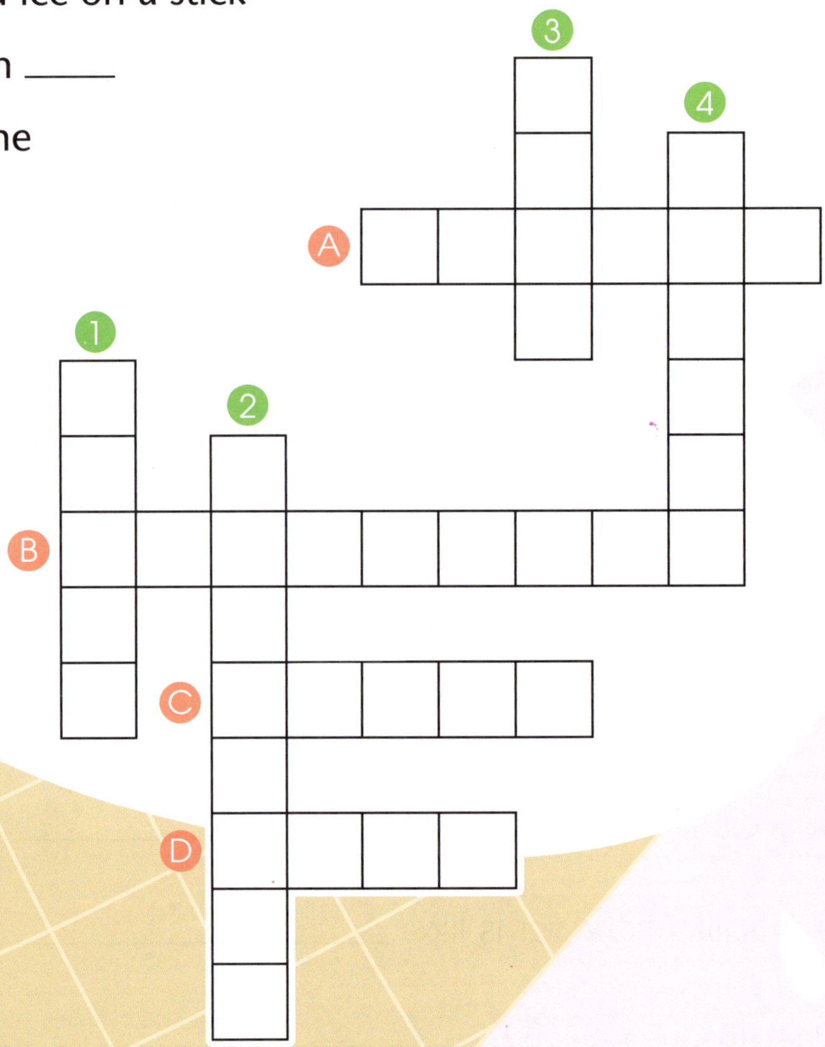

ISBN: 978-1-77149-144-0

D. Solve the riddles.

1. We have no wings but we can fly in the sky.
   Our tails come in various lengths.
   Some of our tails are short and some are long.
   We come in many shapes and colours.
   We love the wind but we hate the rain.

   Guess

2. I'm sweet and nice and brown.
   Everyone likes me.
   I'm usually in good shape, except when it's hot.
   Then I become gooey.
   Still, I remain as sweet as I can be.

   Guess

3. I'm big, tall, and yellow.
   The sun is my best friend.
   I always look at him when he's around.
   People say that I'm beautiful.
   And they find my seeds yummy too.

   Guess

ISBN: 978-1-77149-144-0

A. Name the shapes of the packets and see how many glasses of juice each packet can hold. Then colour the correct answers.

1.

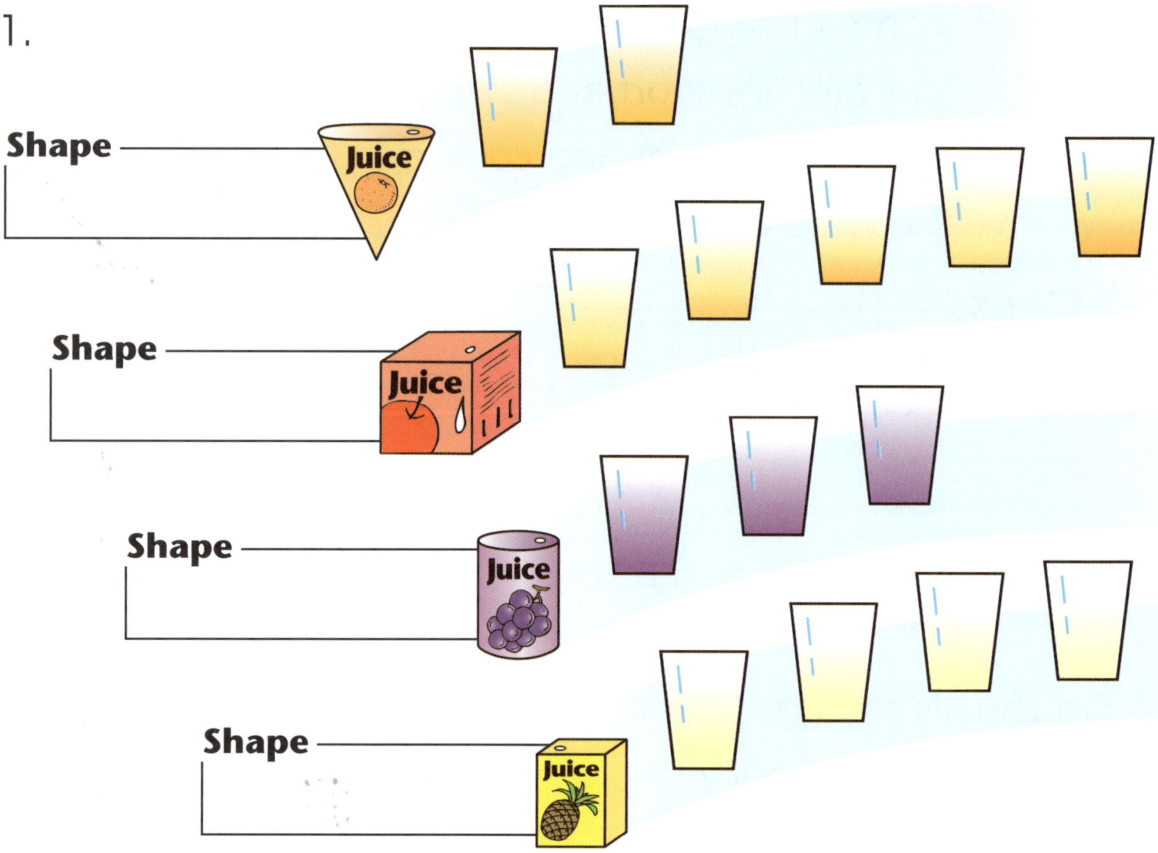

2. holds more

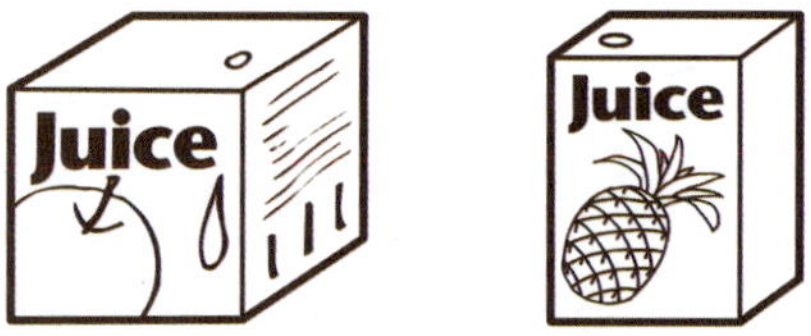

3. holds less

4. greatest capacity: 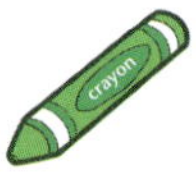

least capacity: 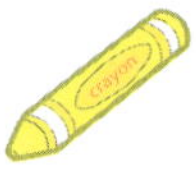

ISBN: 978-1-77149-144-0

B. Colour each container to show how much of it is filled.

1. $\frac{1}{4}$ filled

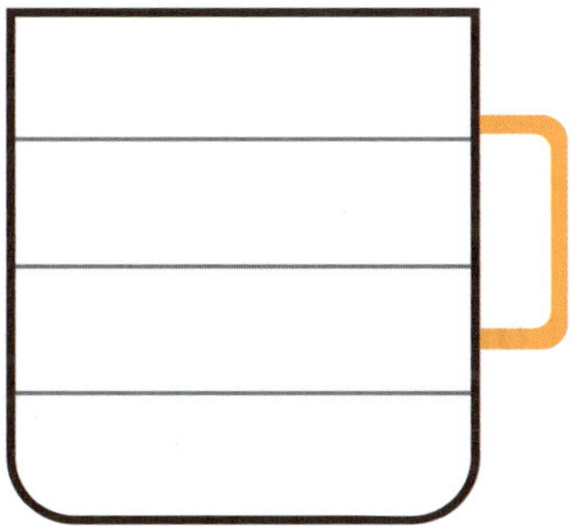

2. $\frac{1}{2}$ filled

3. $\frac{1}{3}$ filled

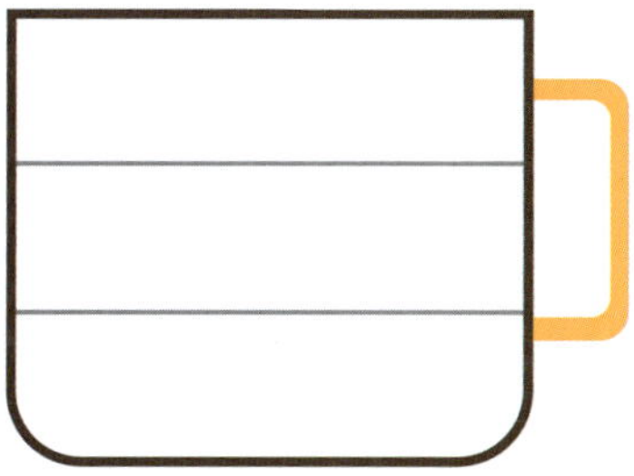

C. Look at the groups of things. Write the fractions.

1.

2.

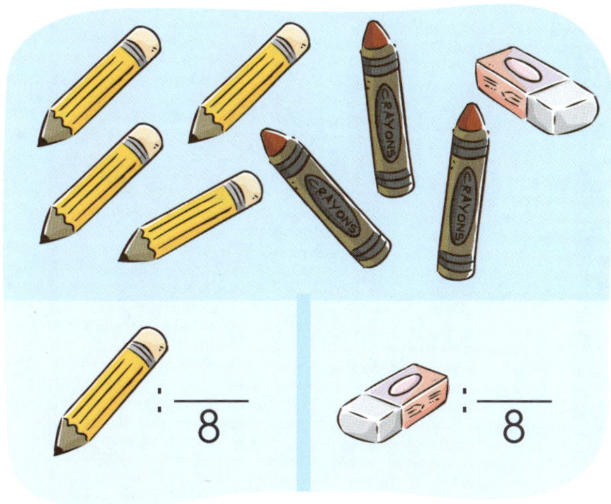

3.

4.

ISBN: 978-1-77149-144-0

Week 3

Mathematics

D. See how much food one child eats at a party. Then draw and write the amount of each kind of food needed to feed 12 children.

1 child eats...

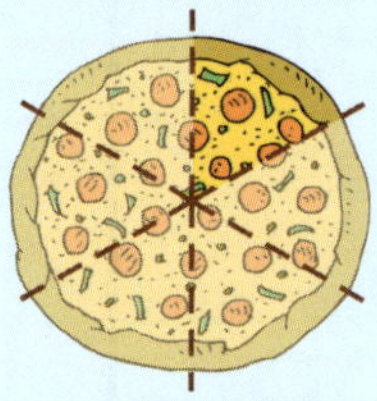

one sixth of a pizza

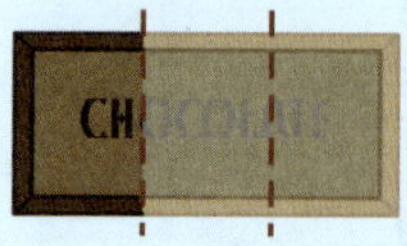

one third of a chocolate bar

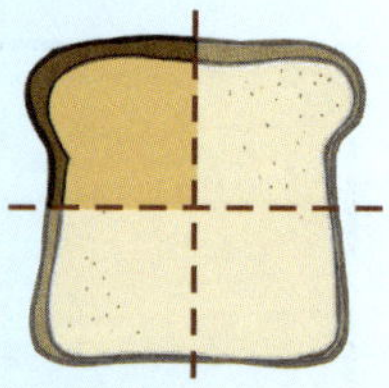

one fourth of a sandwich

12 children eat...

________ 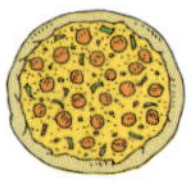

________ 

________ 

ISBN: 978-1-77149-144-0

E. Look at the spinners. Then answer the questions.

1. If Kate spins spinner A, she is likely to get a ________ .

2. If Kate wants a doll, she should spin spinner ________ .

Spinner B is a fair spinner, but spinner A is not.

3. Why does Kate say so?

____

____

____

ISBN: 978-1-77149-144-0

The 3 States of Water

liquid solid gas

A. Solve each riddle.

1. Water in a puddle on a very cold day will become this if left that way.

State ____________

2. Your towels are wet so you hang them on a line. Liquid to this, given sun and time.

State ____________

3. Steam from the shower fills the bathroom with mist. As it hits the mirror, it becomes this.

State ____________

ISBN: 978-1-77149-144-0

B. Fill in the blanks. Then label the boxes in the diagram with the words in bold.

When water **is heated**, it slowly turns into gas, or water 1. ______________ (vapour/perfume), and rises into the 2. ______________ (air/balloon). Clouds are formed when water vapour **condenses** and forms 3. ______________ (rice/water) droplets on dust particles in the air.

ISBN: 978-1-77149-144-0

A. Fill in the blanks. Then answer the question.

English French
ships identity
cultures

The French came to Canada on 1. ____________ . They brought the 2. ____________ language with them.

The British were some of the early settlers. They brought the 3. ____________ language to Canada.

After the settlement of the British and the French, people from all over the world started coming to Canada. They brought with them their unique 4. ____________ and helped shape Canada's 5. ____________ .

List two things that make Canada a good place to live.

____________ ____________

ISBN: 978-1-77149-144-0

B. Match the celebrations with the cultures that celebrate them in Canada. Then answer the question.

(A) 

Easter

(B) 

National Aboriginal Day

(C) 

Thanksgiving Day

1. 

I'm thankful that we have arrived safely. ◯

2. ◯ *As Christians, we have a special day to remember Jesus.*

3. 

Your traditional uses of plants are amazing! ◯

What does Canada celebrate on July 1?

____

ISBN: 978-1-77149-144-0

ISBN: 978-1-77149-144-0

WEEK 4

Arts & Crafts
- make Mexican shakers

Comics
- The Monkey's Heart

Fun Places to Go in Summer
- The African Lion Safari

ISBN: 978-1-77149-144-0

Mexican Shakers

ISBN: 978-1-77149-144-0

Materials:

- toilet paper roll(s)
- rice
- paint
- plastic wrap or foil
- paintbrush
- elastic bands (2 per shaker)

Directions:

1. Paint outside of toilet paper roll.
2. Let it dry. Then decorate it with some beautiful patterns.
3. Cover one end with plastic wrap or foil and secure it with elastic band.
4. Pour about 2 tablespoons of rice into roll.
5. Cover other end of roll and secure it with elastic band.

Have fun shaking your Mexican shakers!

ISBN: 978-1-77149-144-0

COMICS

The Monkey's Heart

ISBN: 978-1-77149-144-0

ISBN: 978-1-77149-144-0

ISBN: 978-1-77149-144-0

ISBN: 978-1-77149-144-0

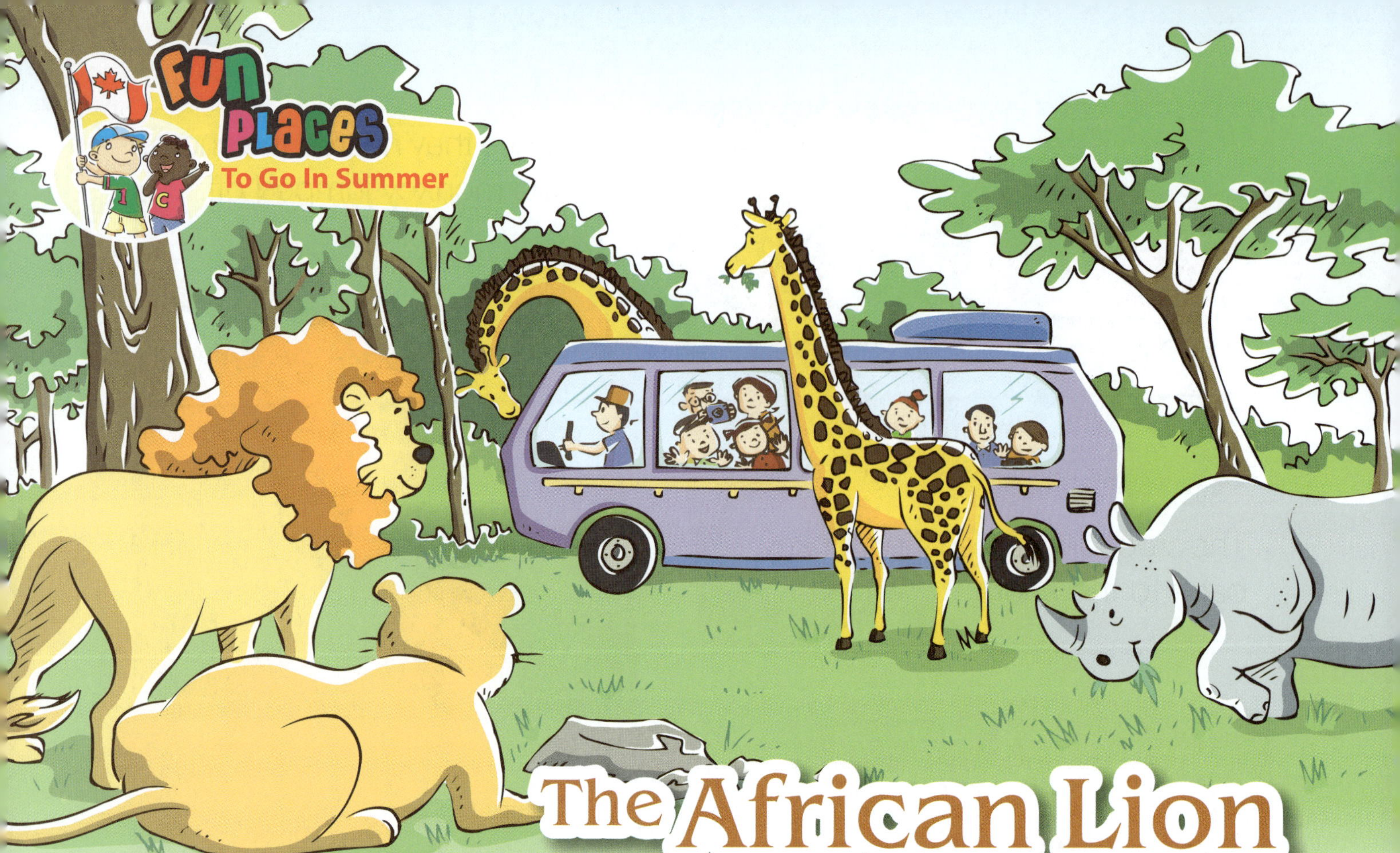

The African Lion Safari

Did you know that you can have an exciting safari experience right here in Canada? Just hop into a car and go to the African Lion Safari in Cambridge, Ontario.

This reserve is home to all kinds of African wild animals. Unlike a zoo, the animals here are not caged or put behind glass. Instead, you can be an adventurer and enter their world: close the doors and windows of your car, and then drive through the different trails. Don't be surprised to see a giraffe next to you, and watch out for the monkeys because they like to jump on cars! For your own safety, and that of the animals, you should never pet or feed the animals.

Enjoy your day by watching the animals eat and play, or catch one of the entertaining animal shows!

ISBN: 978-1-77149-144-0

Week 5

English

- read a story and correct misspelled words
- create lists
- make words with given letters
- match synonyms
- use the plural form

Mathematics

- read a calendar
- choose appropriate measurement units
- find areas of shapes on a grid
- calculate the costs of objects

Science

- learn about the various forms of water
- learn about the ways solids and liquids interact

Social Studies

- match activities with places in Ontario
- learn about places in Ontario and the work there

* The Canadian penny is no longer in circulation. It is used in the unit to show money amounts to the cent.

ISBN: 978-1-77149-144-0

A. **Read the story. There are eight words that are not spelled correctly. Circle them and rewrite them correctly on the lines.**

Two Best Friends

Kyle and Daniel are next door neighbours and they are also best freinds. They spend most of their free time together.

On summor days, the two boys can be found in the feild playing soccer. When the sun gets too hot, the boys clime up to the tree house where they spend their time reeding their favourite comic books. Kyle enjoys reading Spider-Man while Daniel allways picks Superman.

In wintor, both Kyle and Daniel play hockey. They are on the same teem. Kyle is the goalie and Daniel is a forward. They both hope that one day the Toronto Maple Leafs will win the Stanley Cup.

- ____________________
- ____________________
- ____________________
- ____________________
- ____________________
- ____________________
- ____________________
- ____________________

Week 5 English

ISBN: 978-1-77149-144-0

B. Think about your best friend. Write three things on each list.

How we are the same

- ______________________________
- ______________________________
- ______________________________

How we are different

- ______________________________
- ______________________________
- ______________________________

C. Write four words that you can create using the letters in the word "friendship".

f r i e n d s h i p

Examples

end

den

dish

- ______________
- ______________
- ______________
- ______________

ISBN: 978-1-77149-144-0

D. Circle the words in the word search. Then match them with the synonyms.

little glad toss funny caring choose

a	t	n	c	h	o	o	s	e	b
v	n	g	p	m	y	q	l	w	k
b	j	l	i	t	t	l	e	i	t
n	u	a	p	r	o	h	e	q	n
h	j	d	w	n	s	e	h	n	q
f	q	e	b	n	s	k	w	t	b
u	n	a	u	j	y	o	e	b	r
n	b	c	a	r	i	n	g	n	e
n	w	g	t	z	o	l	w	t	b
y	i	h	g	y					
k	b	e							n
e	p	q							w

Synonyms

1. throw ____________
2. small ____________
3. amusing ____________
4. pick ____________
5. kind ____________
6. happy ____________

ISBN: 978-1-77149-144-0

E. Fill in the blanks with the plural form of each noun.

1.

child ______________

2.

deer ______________

3. The dentist cleaned my (tooth) ______________ .

4. She is scared of (mouse) ______________ .

5. Six kids have twelve (foot) ______________ .

6. All the (man) ______________ in the band played the guitar.

7. These (moose) ______________ are crossing the river.

8.

ISBN: 978-1-77149-144-0

Week 5

Mathematics

A. Complete Jane's calendar. Then answer the questions.

1.

Jane's Calendar ______________________

the tenth month of the year

SUN	MON	TUE	WED	THU	FRI	SAT
	1	2			5	
	8		10			13
14			17	18		
21	22	23			26	
		30				

2. Halloween is on ______________ (day of the week).

3. Jane's birthday is on ______________ (date).

4. ______________ (date) is the Sunday before Jane's birthday.

5. Jane goes to the library every Saturday. On what dates does she go to the library?

____

ISBN: 978-1-77149-144-0

B. Write the correct units (m/cm) for each item. Then record the measurements of the sticker album and check ✓ the most appropriate gift bag.

- The fishing rod is about 1 ______ long.
- The string for the kite is about 30 ______ long.
- The string of the yo-yo is about 105 ______ long.

length ______

width ______

Gift bag for the album:

(A)

8 cm

15 cm

(B)

10 cm

5 cm

(C)

8 cm

11 cm

ISBN: 978-1-77149-144-0

C. Record the area of each sticker by counting the number of squares covered. Then answer the questions.

1.

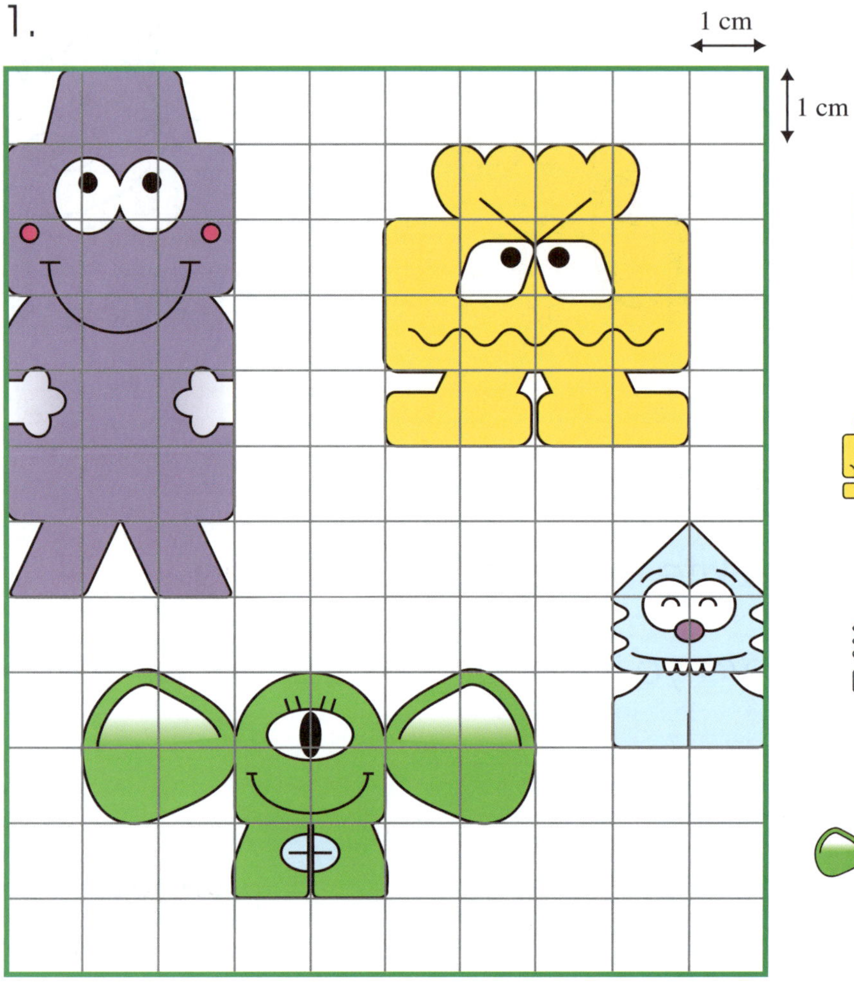

Area

about ______ squares

about ______ squares

about ______ squares

about ______ squares

2a. How many can be put on one page of the album at most?

______

b. How many can be put on one page of the album at most?

______

ISBN: 978-1-77149-144-0

D. Complete the table to show the costs of the stickers. Then answer the questions.

1.

Cost for				
1 sticker				
2 stickers				
3 stickers				
4 stickers				
5 stickers				

2. *Each pack of stickers costs 55¢. If I pay 3 quarters for a pack, what is my change?*

____

3. *If I want to buy 3 stickers of each type, how much will I pay?*

____

ISBN: 978-1-77149-144-0

A. Circle the six water words in the word search and write them on the lines. Then match the words with the pictures.

w	b	e	s	u	i	p	z	d
r	a	i	n	b	c	t	n	e
t	g	k	o	q	e	p	i	w
w	h	r	w	c	l	o	u	d
i	j	b	w	i	y	h	t	e
b	v	a	p	o	u	r	g	b

The first letter of each water word is highlighted.

Water Words

r________ •

s________ •

i________ •

d________ •

c________ •

v________ •

Science Fun

Our bodies are mostly made of water.

ISBN: 978-1-77149-144-0

B. Read what Katie says. Then write the correct descriptions.

Things in Water

dissolves sinks floats

1. sugar in water: ______________

2. cork in water: ______________

3. sand in water: ______________

Water on Things

repelled absorbed

1. water on a sock: ______________
2. water on a towel: ______________
3. water on a raincoat: ______________

ISBN: 978-1-77149-144-0

A. **Different places in Ontario are good for different activities. Match each activity with the correct place.**

Activities

A

B

C

D

1.

farmland near Lake Ontario

2.

Algonquin Provincial Park

3.

Niagara vineyards

4.

Blue Mountain

ISBN: 978-1-77149-144-0

B. Read the descriptions of the places in Ontario. Then match the people with the places where they work.

A factory worker

B tour guide

C chef

Places in Ontario

Dryden

The forests provide wood for building a large paper and pulp industry in this area.

Toronto

A lot of people, with different ethnic backgrounds, live here. They like good food and enjoy the variety of restaurants in this area.

Niagara Falls

A lot of tourists from all over the world visit this area. It is known as one of the world's most beautiful places.

ISBN: 978-1-77149-144-0

ISBN: 978-1-77149-144-0

WEEK 6

English

- read a story
- match synonyms
- write a message
- find antonyms
- choose appropriate homophones

Mathematics

- colour a pictograph
- solve problems using a pictograph
- recognize and complete patterns
- identify transformations

Science

- understand the functions of simple machines
- identify the fulcrums in levers

Social Studies

- learn interesting facts about the City of Toronto
- learn about Toronto's means of transportation

ISBN: 978-1-77149-144-0

A. Read the passage.

A Message in a Bottle

It was a hot summer day. Justin strolled along the shore. He was looking for unusual shells when suddenly he noticed a glass bottle floating in the water. Justin ran quickly and grabbed it when it came close to the shore. There was something inside. It was a piece of paper neatly rolled and tied with a ribbon. Justin cautiously opened the bottle and pulled out the paper. On the paper, the following was written:

Dear Finder,

My name is Emily and I live on beautiful Prince Edward Island. I am sending this message to tell people about my home. An ocean surrounds Prince Edward Island. I am always happy when I smell the salt water and hear the sound of the waves hitting the rocks along the shore. The beaches are a great place for building sandcastles and for finding shells. The sky is blue and filled with many birds. I love my home and hope that one day you could visit my island.

Yours truly,
Emily

ISBN: 978-1-77149-144-0

B. Match each underlined word in the story with its synonym.

1. took ____________
2. curled ____________
3. walked ____________
4. strange ____________
5. carefully ____________
6. detected ____________

Synonyms *are words with similar meanings.*

C. Write a paragraph for a bottle message describing a beautiful place that you would like to share with others.

Dear Finder,

____

____

____

____

____

____

____

____

____

ISBN: 978-1-77149-144-0

Week 6

English

D. Complete the crossword puzzle with the antonyms of the words from the passage.

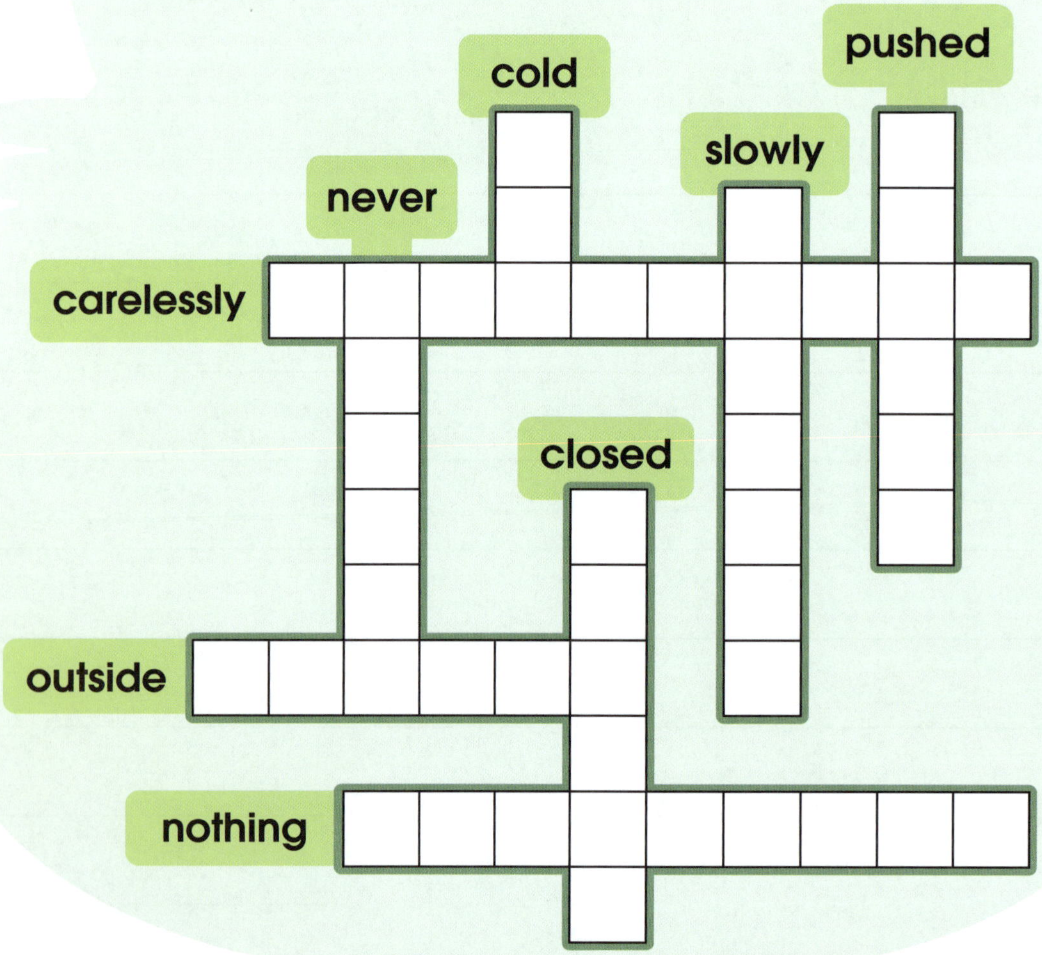

ISBN: 978-1-77149-144-0

E. Fill in the blanks with the correct homophones.

Homophones *are words that sound the same but have different spellings and meanings.*

1. I spent one ____________ vacationing on Prince Edward Island.
   (weak/week)

2. The ____________ circled the airport before landing.
   (plain/plane)

3. Ann wore her ____________ bathing suit to the beach.
   (new/knew)

4. I ____________ enjoy a trip to an island.
   (would/wood)

5. Sam took his boat out to the ____________ .
   (see/sea)

6. The ____________ sky was filled with seagulls.
   (blew/blue)

ISBN: 978-1-77149-144-0

A. **Count and colour the pictograph to show the number of biscuits in the box.**

Number of Biscuits

ISBN: 978-1-77149-144-0

B. Look at the pictograph again. Then answer the questions.

1. How many  and  are there?

   ________ biscuits

2. How many biscuits are there in all?

   ________ biscuits

3. How many biscuits are in the shape of a square?

   ________ biscuits

4. How many biscuits with 4 sides are there?

   ________ biscuits

5. All the biscuits are put equally into 4 bags. How many biscuits are there in each bag?

   ________ biscuits

6. *I paid $1 for this box of biscuits.*

   Draw coins to show her change.

   ________ cents

ISBN: 978-1-77149-144-0

C. **See how many biscuits each child has eaten in the past three days. Follow the pattern to draw the biscuits that each child will eat on Thursday. Then circle the correct words.**

1.

Pattern: growing / shrinking

The number of biscuits increases / decreases by 2 / 3 each day.

2.

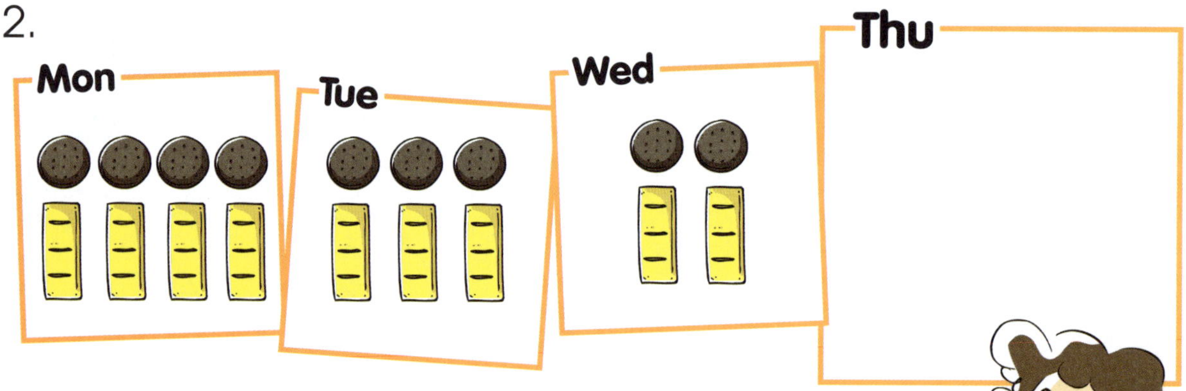

Pattern: growing / shrinking

The number of biscuits increases / decreases by 2 / 3 each day.

ISBN: 978-1-77149-144-0

D. Write the correct words in the arrows to tell how each picture was moved. Then draw to answer the question.

flip turn slide

1.

2.

3.

4. Draw how the picture will look after it is turned to the right.

ISBN: 978-1-77149-144-0

A. **Sort the simple machines. Write the letters.**

Simple Machines

pulley ______

lever ______

wedge ______

screw ______

wheel and axle ______

inclined plane ______

ISBN: 978-1-77149-144-0

B. For each lever, colour the arrow that correctly shows where the fulcrum is.

*The **fulcrum** is the pivot point on a lever. It is the point about which a lever's arm turns.*

ISBN: 978-1-77149-144-0

A. Look at the information about the City of Toronto. Then fill in the blanks.

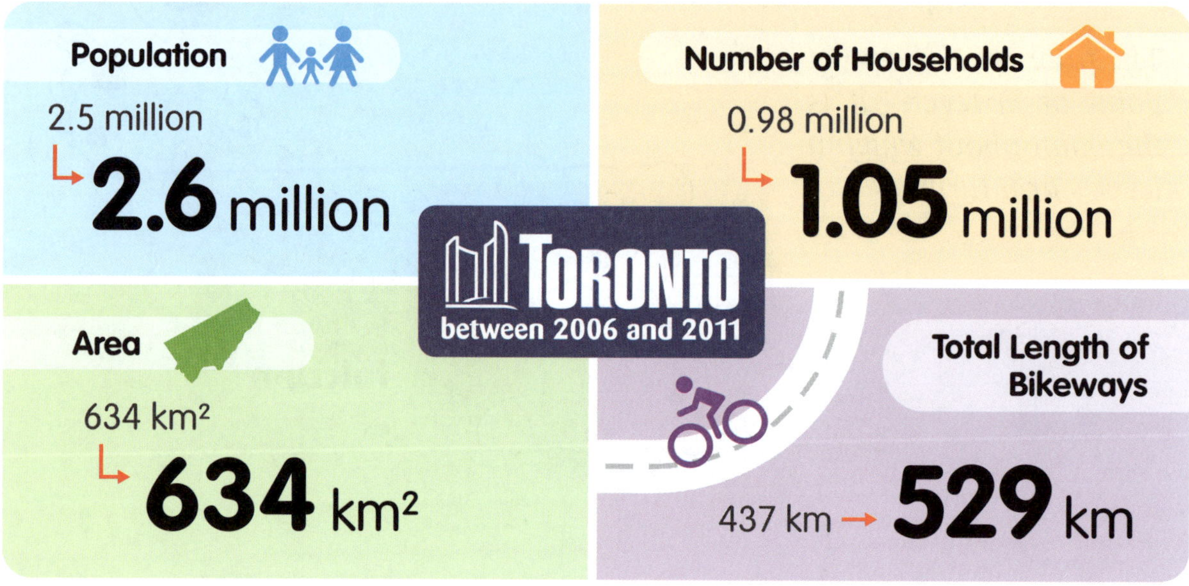

Interesting Facts!

stayed the same
increased
decreased

Between 2006 and 2011:

- Toronto's population ____________ because more people came to live here, and because the number of births increased.
- The number of households in Toronto ____________ because of the city's growing population.
- Toronto's land area ____________ even though the needs of its population increased.
- The length of bikeways ____________ in order to provide accessible routes for Toronto's cyclists and to encourage more people to ride their bikes.

ISBN: 978-1-77149-144-0

B. Label the different means of transportation in the City of Toronto. Then answer the questions.

airplane subway car bike train

by ____________

by ____________

by ____________

by ____________

by ____________

1. Which means of transportation
   a. is the fastest? ____________
   b. is the slowest? ____________
   c. causes no air pollution? ____________

2. Write two advantages of going to school by bike rather than by car.

____

ISBN: 978-1-77149-144-0

ISBN: 978-1-77149-144-0

Week 7

English

- read a story and put the events in order
- write an ending to a story
- complete a crossword puzzle
- put words in order to make sentences

Mathematics

- identify positions on a map
- calculate costs
- do addition and multiplication to solve problems
- read the time on clocks

Science

- learn about movements
- understand forces and the direction of movements

Social Studies

- learn about Canada's boreal forest
- learn about deforestation

ISBN: 978-1-77149-144-0

Week

7

English

A. Read the story. Then put the events in order from 1 to 4.

Bottom of the Ninth

"Strike two!" yelled the umpire.

It was the bottom of the ninth inning and Kenny's team, the Sluggers, was tied with the Hurricanes. There were two outs. Kenny knew that he had to hit the ball so that his team could win the championship. He tried to stay calm but sweat kept running down his back.

Kenny squeezed the bat tightly and stared at the pitcher on the mound. The catcher was signalling to the pitcher. The pitcher was rolling the baseball around in his black mitt dreaming of a strike out. Suddenly he threw the ball. Kenny watched the ball as it came toward home plate.

◯ The score was tied between the Sluggers and the Hurricanes.

◯ The catcher was signalling to the pitcher.

◯ The pitcher suddenly threw the ball.

◯ Kenny started to sweat.

ISBN: 978-1-77149-144-0

B. Write an ending to the story and give it a new title.

Your ending can be exciting, unexpected, or just plain funny.

New Title: ____________________

Kenny watched the ball as it came toward home plate.

____

____

____

____

____

____

____

____

____

______________________ **The End**

ISBN: 978-1-77149-144-0

C. **Read the clues and complete the crossword puzzle with baseball words from the passage.**

Across

A. glove
B. He squats behind the batter.
C. The runner has to touch this to score.
D. a round in the game
E. where the pitcher stands

Down

1. He throws the ball.
2. club for hitting the ball
3. baseball referee
4. being the winning team

ISBN: 978-1-77149-144-0

D. Put these words in order to make sentences. Include capital letters and periods.

***Capital letters** are used at the beginning of sentences.*

***Periods** are used at the end of sentences.*

There is a baseball field beside my school**.**

1. fun play baseball sport is to a

2. it day summer was hot a

3. team finally won our

4. we lemonade after drank game the

5. cheered ball the she crowd as the hit

1. ______________________________

2. ______________________________

3. ______________________________

4. ______________________________

5. ______________________________

ISBN: 978-1-77149-144-0

A. Look at the map of the City Zoo. Help the children find their way to different spots and fill in the blanks.

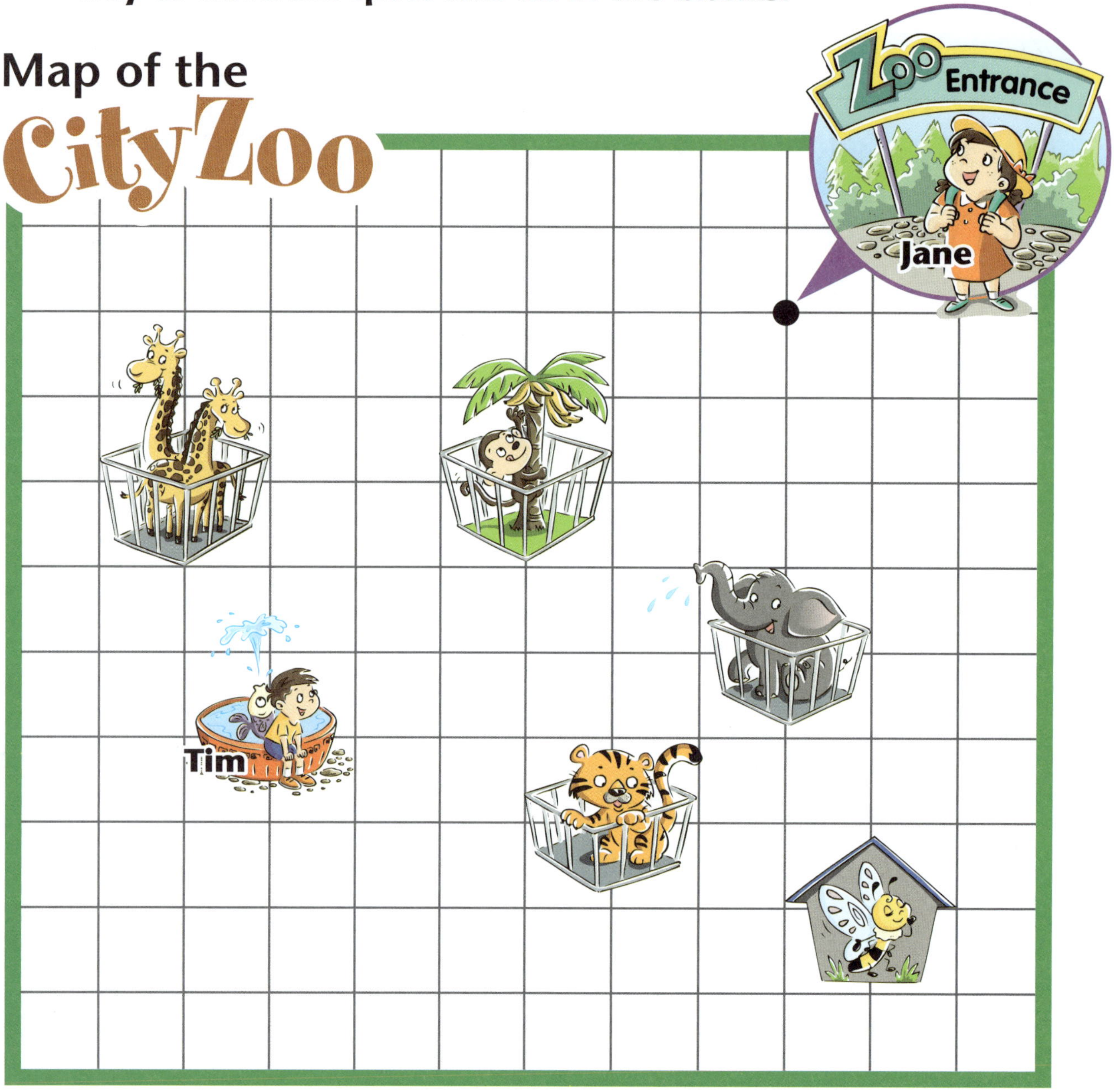

1. Jane wants to see the monkeys.

   She should go ______ block(s) to the ____________ (left/right) and ______ block(s) ____________ (up/down) .

2. Tim wants to see the giraffes. He should go ____________

   ____ .

ISBN: 978-1-77149-144-0

3.

Which way should I go from the giraffes to the Butterfly House?

He should go ______________________________

______________________________ .

4.

I'm watching the tigers. If I go 2 blocks to the right and 2 blocks up, what will I see?

She will see ______________ .

5. *If an adult pays $50 for 1 ticket, how much is the change?*

______ ◯ ______ = ______

The change is $ ______ .

6. How much do the tickets for two children cost?

______ ◯ ______ = ______

The tickets cost $ ______ .

ISBN: 978-1-77149-144-0

B. Draw the pictures and fill in the missing numbers to solve the problems.

Each child has...

2 (banana) to feed the monkeys.	3 (cup) of grain to feed the giraffes.	5 (leaf) to feed the elephants.

1

5 children have ______ (banana) in all.

2

4 children have ______ (cup) in all.

3

3 children have ______ (leaf) in all.

ISBN: 978-1-77149-144-0

C. Help Jack write the arrival time at different spots. Then answer the questions.

1.

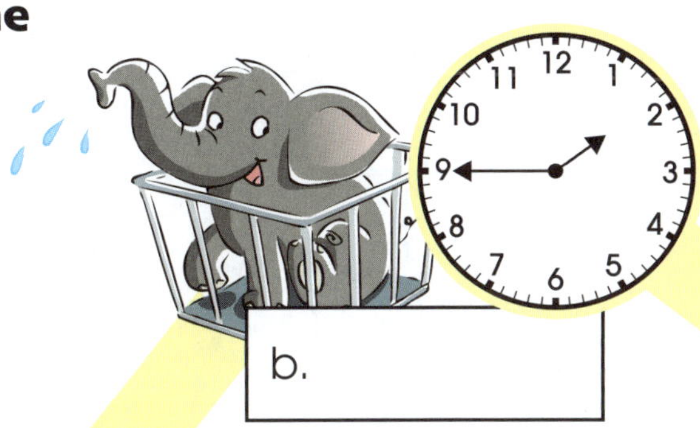

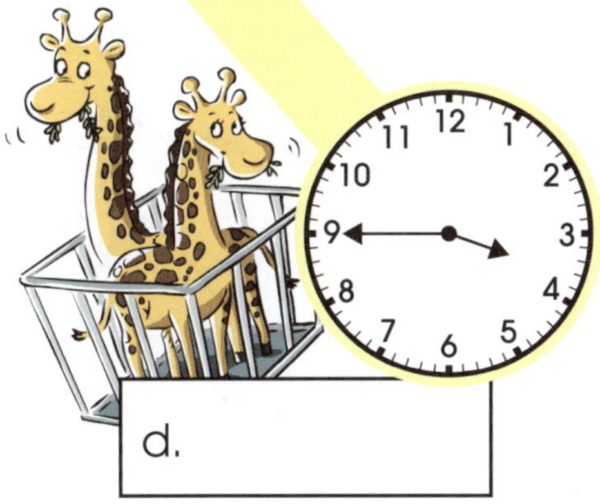

2. Jack left home at 10:45 a.m. to go to the zoo. How long did it take him to get there?

____

3. The zoo opens at 10:00 a.m. and closes at 8:00 p.m. For how many hours is it open?

____

4. Jack spent 30 minutes at the Butterfly House. What time did he leave the House? Draw the clock hands to show the time.

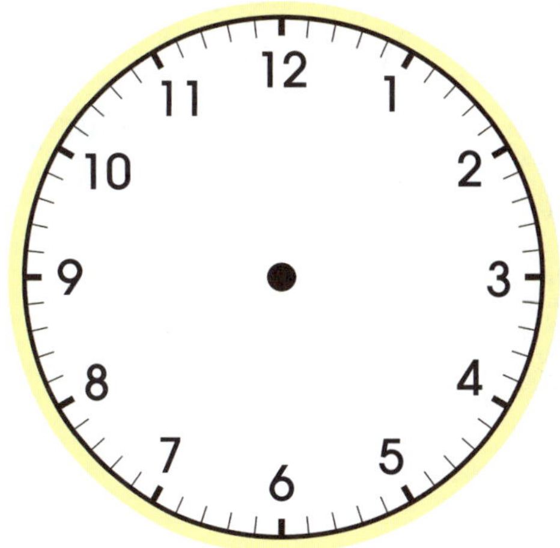

ISBN: 978-1-77149-144-0

A. Circle the word that describes each movement.

rolling / swinging

spinning / sliding

turning / swinging

bouncing / sliding

swinging rolling

ISBN: 978-1-77149-144-0

B. Trace the arrow to show the direction of movement in each scene. Then write whether each object is being "pushed" or "pulled" and answer the question.

Push or Pull

***Movement** only happens if a force is acting on an object or body. A force can be a push or a pull.*

1.

apples ____________

2.

boy ____________

3.

table ____________

4.

Which objects in the pictures above are moving because of gravity?

____

ISBN: 978-1-77149-144-0

A. **Read the paragraph about the boreal forest in Canada. Then complete the crossword puzzle using words from the paragraph.**

Canada has a lot of natural resources. We should be careful how we use them.

The Boreal Forest

The boreal forest is the largest forest region in Canada. It runs across the country from west to east, and makes up a big area of Canada's total forests. The boreal forest plays the important role of providing a natural habitat for animals and plants. It also provides us with valuable resources like wood and fresh air.

It is our home.

The boreal forest – the ________ forest region in Canada

a resource the forest provides for us

ISBN: 978-1-77149-144-0

B. Circle the correct words to learn about deforestation.

Reasons

Deforestation means cutting down trees in a forest to:

- make room for **buildings / animals** .
- get **wood / food** for human use.

Parts of Canada's forests are cut down to meet human needs. This impacts the environment and resources of the forests.

Impacts

Deforestation can:

- destroy the habitats of **humans / wild animals** .
- **take away / enrich** the natural resources that forests provide for us.

Restoration

To limit the negative effects of deforestation, we should:

- plant as many **trees / flowers** as we cut down.
- limit our use of forest land and use our resources **carelessly / carefully** .

ISBN: 978-1-77149-144-0

ISBN: 978-1-77149-144-0

Arts & Crafts

- make a Chinese dragon

Comics

- King Midas

Fun Places to Go in Summer

- The Radium Hot Springs

ISBN: 978-1-77149-144-0

CHINESE DRAGON

ISBN: 978-1-77149-144-0

Materials:

- 1 cardboard egg carton
- paintbrush
- string
- black pipe cleaners
- glue
- paper bag
- newspaper strips
- red, orange, black, and white construction paper
- orange paint
- elastic band
- scissors

Directions:

1. Cut egg carton in half.
2. Paint it orange. Let it dry.
3. Tie the two rows together with string.
4. Stuff paper bag with newspaper strips.
5. Paint bag orange. Let it dry.
6. Trace parts to make the dragon head on construction paper in different colours.
7. Cut out and glue all pieces in place as shown.
8. Make two small holes below the dragon's nose and add black pipe cleaners.
9. Tie egg carton to paper bag with elastic band.
10. Glue dragon head to paper bag.

ISBN: 978-1-77149-144-0

Comics

King Midas

Once there was a king who lived in Greece. His name was Midas.

One day, the king found a satyr sleeping in his garden.

King Midas knew the satyr's master. He was a powerful god.

ISBN: 978-1-77149-144-0

ISBN: 978-1-77149-144-0

King Midas got his wish. He touched a stone and it turned to gold.

The king was very excited. He touched everything in his palace. All of it turned to gold!

The king was hungry. But when he picked up some food, it turned to gold too.

ISBN: 978-1-77149-144-0

The princess visited her father. She bent down to give him a kiss.

King Midas was very sad. He went to the god.

The End

ISBN: 978-1-77149-144-0

The Radium Hot Springs

This summer, brave the rapids of the Kootenay River in British Columbia by going whitewater rafting!

From Radium Hot Springs, B.C., you will begin an adventure that will get your heart racing. Whitewater rafting involves paddling through thunderous waters on an inflatable boat with a group of people and a guide. So strap on your life jacket and prepare to be jostled around by the roaring rapids as you make your way along the Kootenay. The feeling is exhilarating!

This experience is also breathtaking because of the natural beauty of the area. Take the time to appreciate the beauty of the wilderness and the Canadian Rockies. You can even try to spot some wildlife!

Afterwards, why not take a swim in a hot spring? It would be a nice, relaxing end to a thrilling summer day.

ISBN: 978-1-77149-144-0

Answers

Grades 2-3

Credits

Photos ("children" Gennadiy Poznyakov/123RF.com, "beach" Alexandr Ozerov/123RF.com)

ISBN: 978-1-77149-144-0

ANSWERS

Week 1

English

A. 1. ✔ 2.
3. 4. ✔
5. ✔ 6. ✔

B. (Suggested answers)
1. chips 2. at the cinema
3. cotton 4. snow
5. (Individual answer)

C. pot ; not ; spot ; trot ; dot
drop ; mop ; crop ; shop ; stop

D. bedroom ; basketball ; backpack ; raincoat ; cupcake ; eyelid ; campsite

E. (Suggested answers)
1. sunlight ; sunflower ; sunshine
2. bookmark ; bookstore ; bookshelf

F.

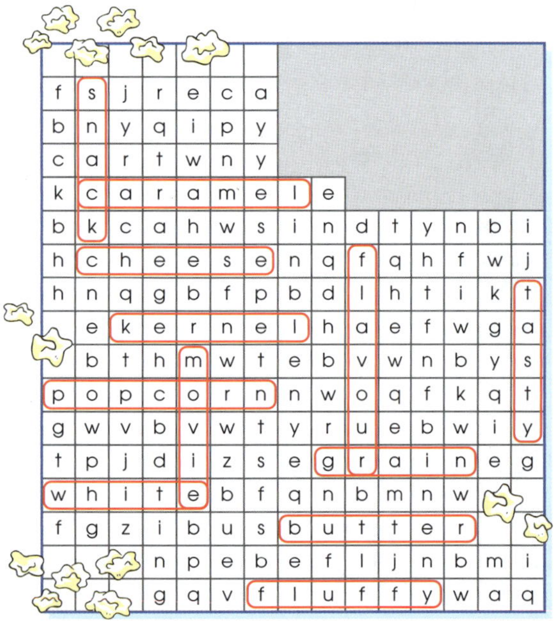

Mathematics

A. 1. 39 2. 66
3. 40 4. 47
5. 51 6. 34
7.

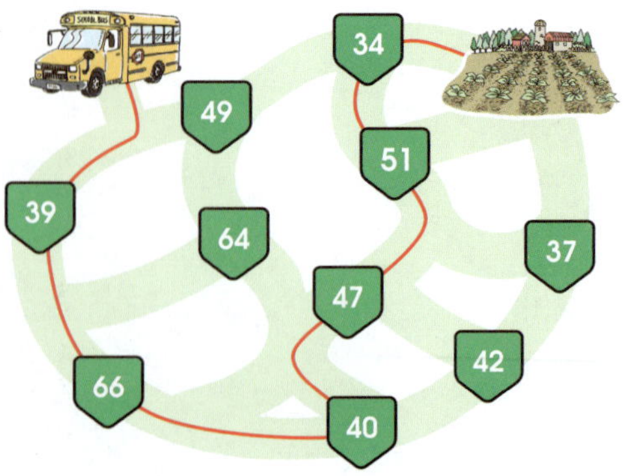

B.1a. 19 + 24 = 43 ; 43
b. 43 – 26 = 17 ; 17
2a. 28 + 28 = 56 ; 56
b. 56 – 43 = 13 ; 13

C. 1. 2 2. 15
3. 24 4. 5

D. A:

The position of the blue bead shifts to the right by 1 each time.

B:

The number of beads increases by 1 each time.

Science

A.

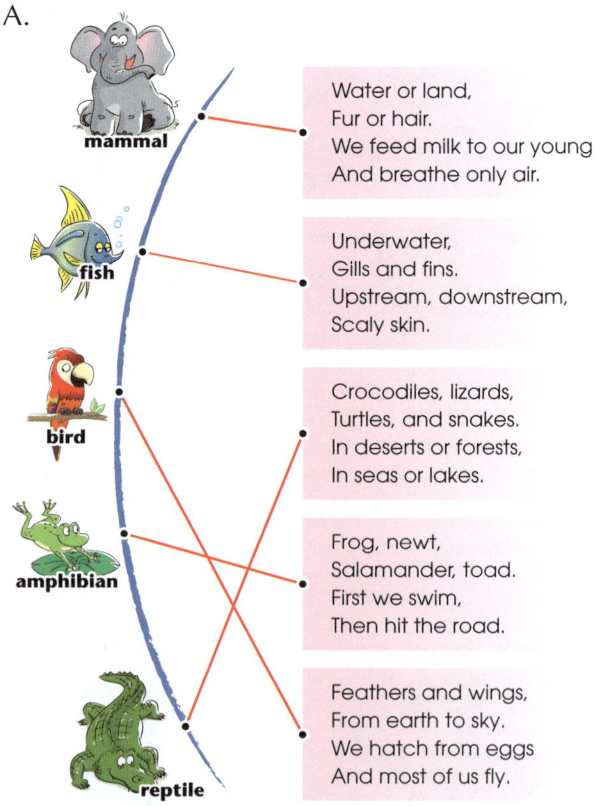

ISBN: 978-1-77149-144-0

B. 1. camouflage ; hibernate ; migrate
   2a. migrate
   b. hibernate
   c. camouflage

Social Studies

A. 1. fishing
   2. protect
   3. nuts
   4. wood
   (Individual drawing and writing)

B.

Week 2

English

A. a red nose ; a hat that is yellow ; shoes that are too big ; a wig ; a painted smile ; baggy clothes that are out of style
   1. A   2. B

B. 1. big   2. clown
   3. way/day   4. face
   5. funny   6. fellow

C. (Individual questions)

D. (Individual name)

E. (Individual writing)

Mathematics

A.

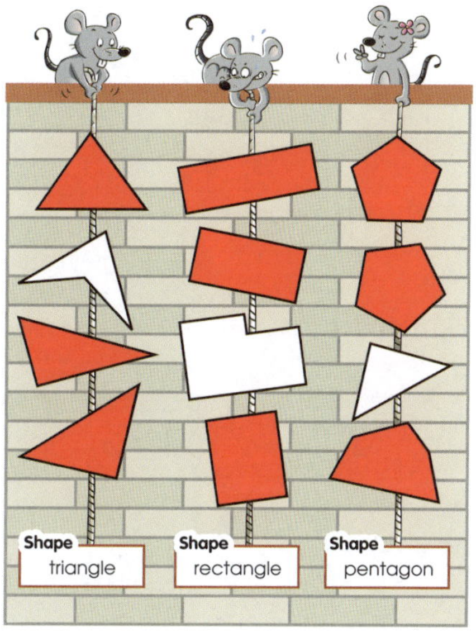

B. 1.

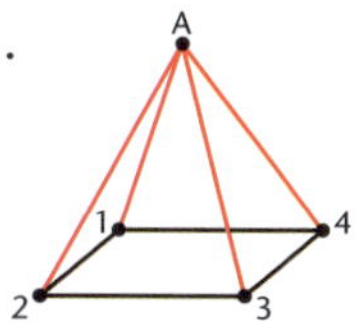

rectangular pyramid ; No

2.

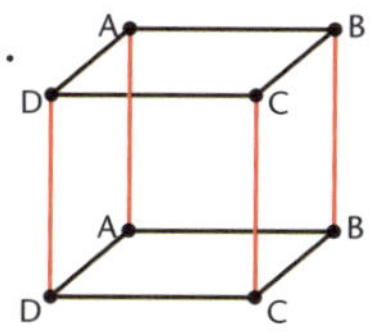

cube ; No

3.

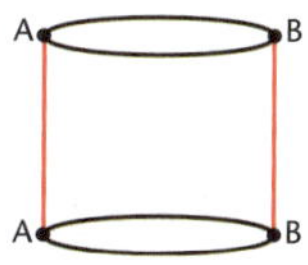

cylinder ; Yes

4.

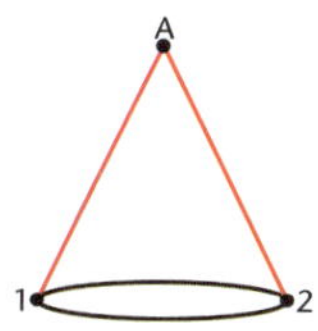

cone ; No

C. 1.

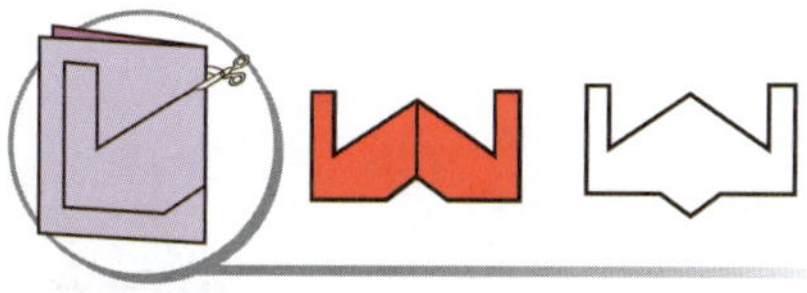

2.

3.

4.

ISBN: 978-1-77149-144-0

D.

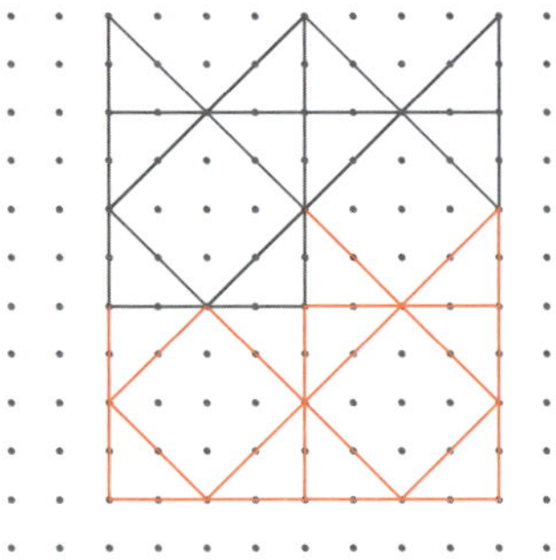

square ; triangle

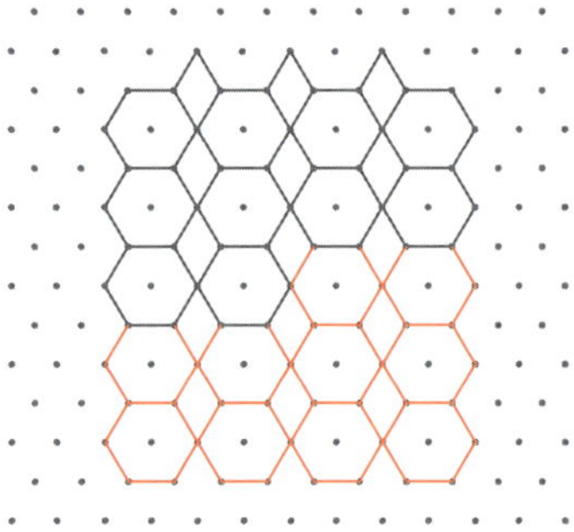

rhombus ; hexagon

Science

A. 1. change
   2. waste
   3. reproduce
   4. food
   5. grow

B. 1. fawn ; deer
   2. kitten ; cat
   3. calf ; cow
   4. piglet ; pig
   5. kid ; goat
   6. cub ; bear

Social Studies

A.

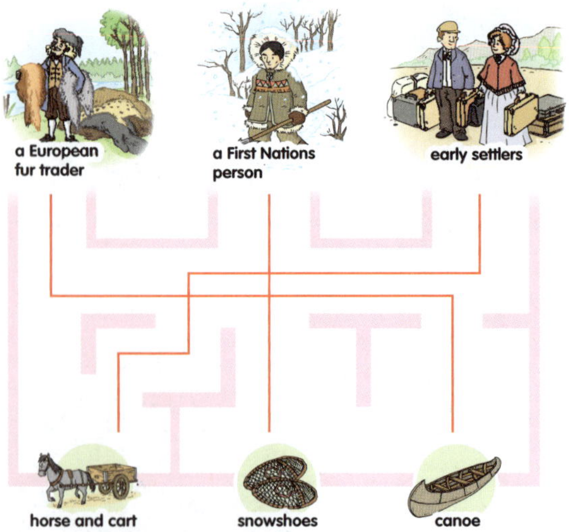

(Individual answer)

B. 1. loads
   2. Canada
   3. bark

big ; lightweight ; abundantly

Week 3

English

A. ice cream

B. (Individual drawing and answers)

C.

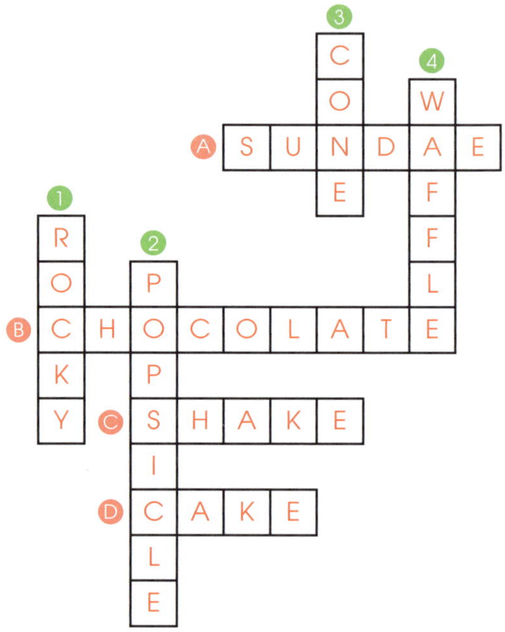

D. 1. kites
   2. chocolate
   3. a sunflower

Mathematics

A. 1. cone ; cube ; cylinder ; rectangular prism

2.

3.

4.

ISBN: 978-1-77149-144-0

B. 1. 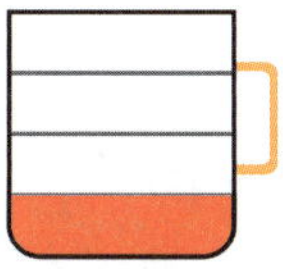

2. 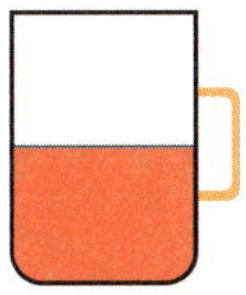

3. 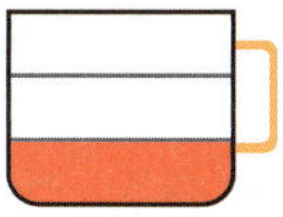

C. 1.

2.

3.

4.

D.

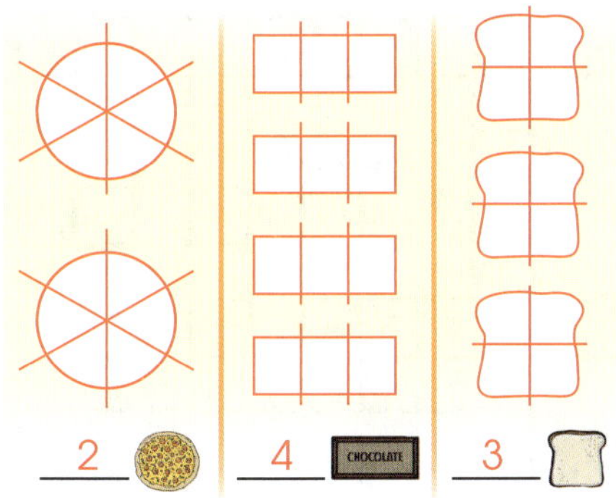

E. 1. top
2. A
3. Spinner B gives you an equal chance of getting one of the three prizes. With spinner A, you are more likely to get a top.

Science

A. 1. solid
2. gas
3. liquid

B. 1. vapour
2. air
3. water
4. condenses
5. is heated

Social Studies

A. 1. ships
2. French
3. English
4. cultures
5. identity
(Individual answers)

B. 1. C
2. A
3. B
Canada Day

Week 5

English

A. (Circle these misspelled words.)
freinds ; summor ; feild ; clime ; reeding ; allways ; wintor ; teem
Correct spellings:
friends ; summer ; field ; climb ; reading ; always ; winter ; team

B. (Individual answers)

C. (Suggested answers)
ship ; send ; fried ; ride

D.

a	t	n	c	h	o	o	s	e	b
v	n	g	p	m	y	q	l	w	k
b	j	l	i	t	t	l	e	i	t
n	u	a	p	r	o	h	e	q	n
h	j	d	w	n	s	e	h	n	q
f	q	e	b	n	s	k	w	t	b
u	n	a	u	j	y	o	e	b	r
n	b	c	a	r	i	n	g	n	e
n	w	g	t	z	o	l	w	t	b
y	i	h	g	y					
k	b	e							
e	p	q							

1. toss
2. little
3. funny
4. choose
5. caring
6. glad

E. 1. children
2. deer
3. teeth
4. mice
5. feet
6. men
7. moose
8. geese

Mathematics

A. 1.

2. Wednesday
3. October 16
4. October 14

ISBN: 978-1-77149-144-0

5. on October 6, October 13, October 20, and October 27

B. m ; m ; cm ; 10 cm ; 7 cm
Check: C

C. 1. 19 ; 14 ; 5 ; 12
2a. 3 b. 2

D. 1.

Cost for	5¢	4¢	2¢	3¢
1 sticker	5¢	4¢	2¢	3¢
2 stickers	10¢	8¢	4¢	6¢
3 stickers	15¢	12¢	6¢	9¢
4 stickers	20¢	16¢	8¢	12¢
5 stickers	25¢	20¢	10¢	15¢

2. 20 cents 3. 42 cents

Science

A.

w	b	e	s	u	i	p	z	d
r	a	i	n	b	c	t	n	e
t	g	k	o	q	e	p	i	w
w	h	r	w	c	l	o	u	d
i	j	b	w	i	y	h	t	e
b	v	a	p	o	u	r	g	b

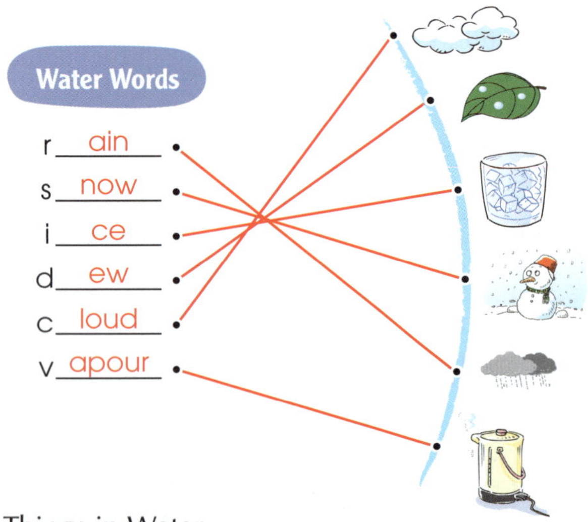

B. Things in Water:
1. dissolves 2. floats
3. sinks

Water on Things:
1. absorbed 2. absorbed
3. repelled

Social Studies

A. 1. D 2. C
3. A 4. B

B. Dryden: A Toronto: C
Niagara Falls: B

Week 6

English

B. 1. grabbed 2. rolled
3. strolled 4. unusual
5. cautiously 6. noticed

C. (Individual writing)

D.

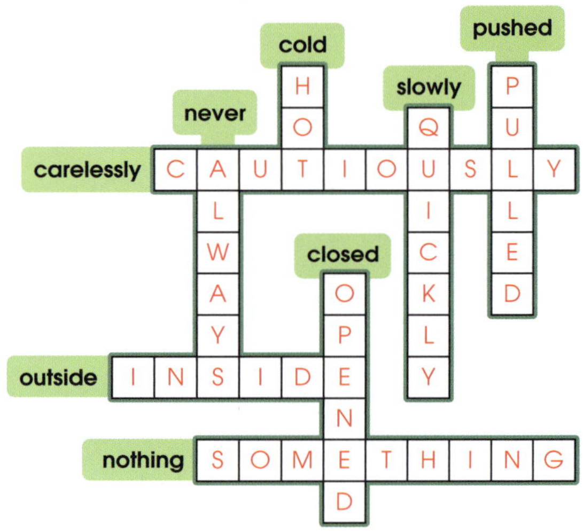

E. 1. week 2. plane
3. new 4. would
5. sea 6. blue

Mathematics

A.

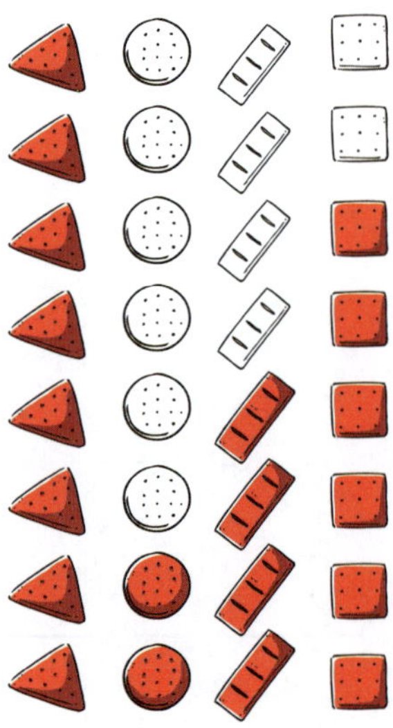

ISBN: 978-1-77149-144-0

B. 1. 10   2. 20
3. 6   4. 10
5. 5
6.

15 cents

C. 1.

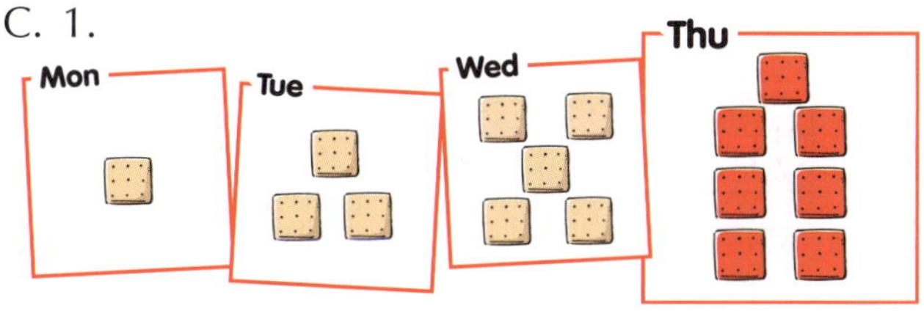

growing ; increases ; 2

2.

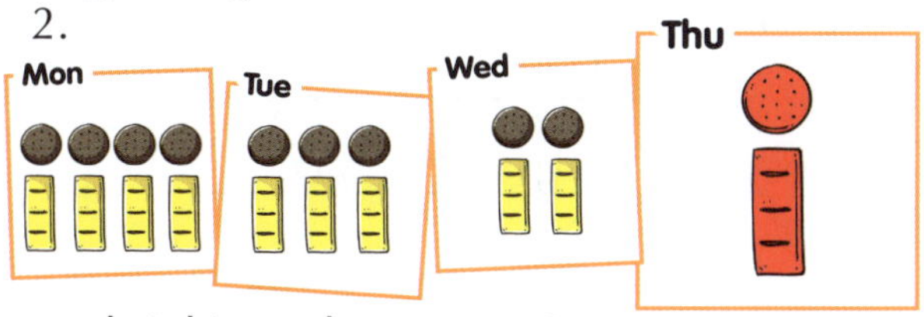

shrinking ; decreases ; 2

D. 1. turn ; slide   2. slide ; turn
3. turn ; flip
4.

Science

A. pulley: B, E
lever: C, H
wedge: D
screw: F
wheel and axle: A, G
inclined plane: I

B.

Social Studies

A. increased ; increased ; stayed the same ; increased

B.

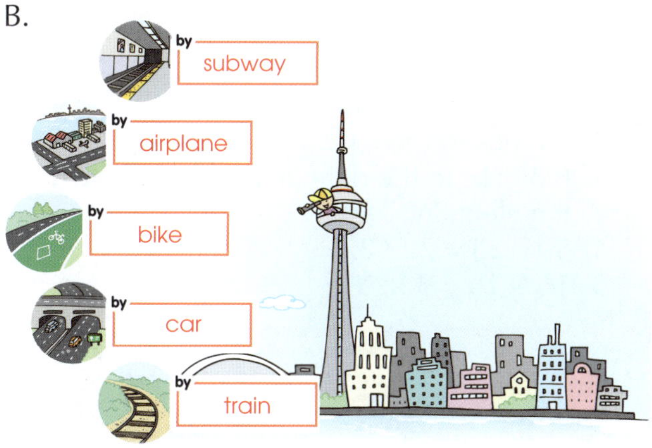

1a. airplane   b. bike
c. bike
2. It is good exercise and it causes no air pollution.

Week 7

English

A. 1 ; 3 ; 4 ; 2
B. (Individual writing)
C.

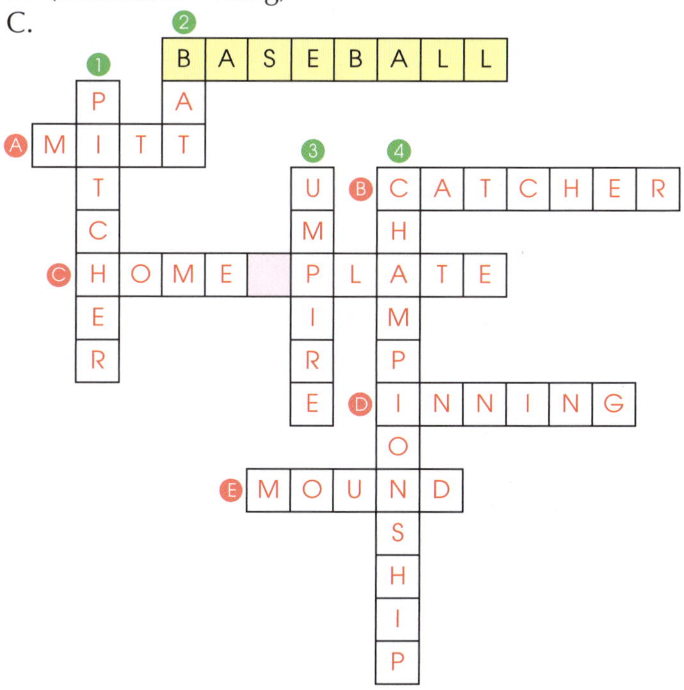

D. 1. Baseball is a fun sport to play.
2. It was a hot summer day.

ISBN: 978-1-77149-144-0

3. Our team finally won. / Our team won finally.
4. We drank lemonade after the game.
5. The crowd cheered as she hit the ball.

Mathematics

A. 1. 3 ; left ; 2 ; down
   2. 1 block to the left and 3 blocks up
   3. 8 blocks to the right and 5 blocks down
   4. the elephants
   5. 50 – 28 = 22 ; 22
   6. 16 + 16 = 32 ; 32

B.

C. 1a. 11:15 a.m.
   b. 1:45 p.m.
   c. 2:30 p.m.
   d. 3:45 p.m.
   2. 30 minutes
   3. 10 hours
   4.

Science

A. toilet paper: rolling
   fan: spinning
   faucet: turning
   clock: swinging
   ball: bouncing

B. (Trace the arrows.)
   1. pulled
   2. pulled
   3. pushed
   4. the apples and the boy

Social Studies

A.

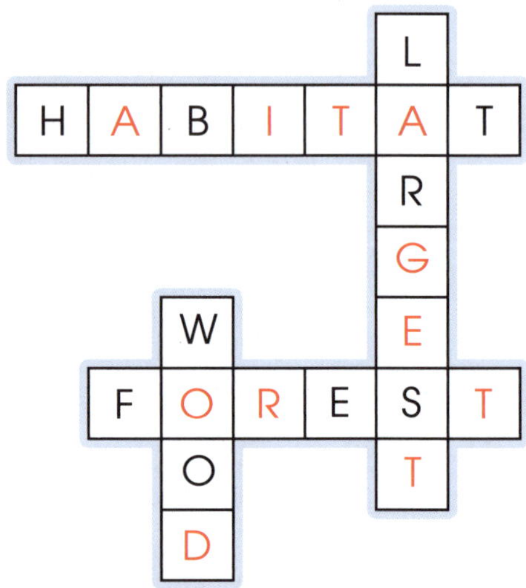

B. Reasons: buildings ; wood
   Impacts: wild animals ; take away
   Restoration: trees ; carefully

ISBN: 978-1-77149-144-0